WHEN I PUT OUT TO SEA

Nicolette Milnes Walker was born in Cheshire in 1943, the fourth daughter of a surgeon. She was educated at Farrington's School, Chislehurst, Kent, and at the University of Bristol, where she gained a BSc degree in Psychology in 1964, and an MSc degree in 1970. She worked first in the University of Bristol, studying the way in which people understand engineering drawings, and then joined the British Aircraft Association's Human Factors Group at Bristol.

In 1970 she went to the University of Wales Institute of Science and Technology in Cardiff, where she participated in studies of repetitive light work in industry.

Her interest in sailing was aroused by a dinghy sailing holiday in Salcombe in 1966 and she built herself a dinghy which she sailed mainly at Weston-super-Mare. She made her first ocean passage as one of a crew of three in a twenty-five-foot boat, which sailed from England to Spain and the Azóres, and back.

CONDITIONS OF SALE

WHEN I PUT OUT TO SEA

NICOLETTE MILNES WALKER

UNABRIDGED

PAN BOOKS LTD : LONDON

First published 1972 by William Collins, Sons and Co Ltd
This edition published 1973 by Pan Books Ltd,
33 Tothill Street, London SW1

ISBN 0 330 23795 0

Printed and Bound in England by
Hazell Watson & Viney Ltd
Aylesbury, Bucks

Contents

List of Illustrations

(Between pages 72 and 73)

Colour photographs by the author

Acknowledgements

The author is grateful to Elizabeth Jennings
for permission to print her poem *Power*; and to
the Trustees of the Estate of the late James
Elroy Flecker, and William Heinemann Limited,
for their permission to use two stanzas from
Hassan.

We are the Pilgrims, master; we shall go
   Always a little further: it may be
Beyond that last blue mountain barred with snow
   Across that angry or that glimmering sea,

White on a throne or guarded in a cave
   There lives a prophet who can understand
Why men were born: but surely we are brave,
   Who take the Golden Road to Samarkand.

From *Hassan*,
by James Elroy Flecker

1　*Why?*

At 11.15 hours on 12 June 1971 I left behind the village of
Dale, sailed past St Ann's Head, almost the extreme south-west
point of Wales, and set off alone in my thirty-foot sloop *Aziz* to
brave the Atlantic Ocean, and a journey of 4,000 miles.

Forty-four and a half days later I arrived in Newport, Rhode
Island, and first set foot in the New World.

Because I was the only woman to have succeeded in crossing
the Atlantic non-stop and alone, my arrival made a small splash
in history. My first reaction when I stepped ashore and found
myself surrounded by welcoming and friendly newspapermen
was to dismiss the past six weeks, forget all the difficulties, put
it all out of my mind and give myself entirely to whatever was to
come (an exhausting but marvellous series of parties, interviews and receptions). Indeed, I could not remember what had
happened and so what the world first learned about my voyage
hardly approached the truth. Then I started to read my diary
and listen to the tape-recordings I had made and the memories
flooded back, about what had happened and how I had felt
about what I was doing.

Why had I gone? I first realized that I was seriously considering
a single-handed crossing of the Atlantic early in 1971, six
months before I in fact set out. I was at the International Boat
Show in London and I found myself secretly looking at all
those exciting pieces of gear that mean so much to sailing
people. I had, as a game I thought, made comprehensive lists of
stores, chandlery and the like which would be needed for such
a crossing. It was fun going through the lists published by various voyagers, comparing them with what I thought necessary

and seeing where we differed. Of course this inevitably led me to look at the types of gear which might be best suited to my needs. This led me to a detailed consideration of the implications of such a voyage. And before I knew where I was it was all planned.

I was like someone whose eye has been caught by a new car. It looks rather nice so you think you will find out a bit more about it. Then you compare it with other cars and it is much more desirable. Then you happen to be passing the showroom. You might as well go in and have a proper look. Well, why shouldn't you have one? You can't get it out of your head. You just have to have that car. So you buy it.

I bought myself a transatlantic voyage.

Well, why not? Obviously the first consideration was financial. Could I pay for everything? If I cashed all my assets I could afford to buy a boat for about £3,000, pay for the extra gear it might need, and still have a bit left over for contingencies.

The second consideration was time. Should I go this year? My job as a research psychologist was due to end in August, but that was clearly too late for a crossing that year, for the hurricane season would have started and the western Atlantic could get very rough. What about next year? Why not enter the Single-handed Transatlantic Race? Because I was not interested in coming way down the field. I could not afford a boat big enough to win. And if I could afford one I doubted I could handle it.

Besides, if I entered that race I could not be sure of being the first woman to make the crossing non-stop. I wanted to be the first for I knew that such an achievement would be very satisfying in many ways.

I am a psychologist by training and I have been concerned with studying the performance of various physical and mental tasks under physically difficult conditions. I had read the books of single-handed sailors and was interested to find out what it really is like to be alone at sea, depending for survival only on oneself.

I do not enjoy conflicts with people, but it gives me great

pleasure to test myself against the world and survive through my own skill. If I win the elements are not hurt. If I lose I alone am hurt. Whatever happens, the suffering and the satisfaction are mine alone and I would not invite anyone to share the risk or the glory. I wanted to make this crossing on my own so that the outcome would depend only on my skill, or lack of it, my willpower, or lack of it – on me.

Could I do it? How many of the millions of women in the world would even consider trying this journey? A thousand? Ten? None? One woman had crossed the Atlantic alone. Ann Davison arrived in the West Indies in 1953, having gone by way of Spain and the Canary Isles. Another, a German named Edith Baumann, had tried the non-stop crossing. Her boat broke up off the Azores and she and a little dog were picked from the sea after taking to her life raft. She escaped with her life. Could I escape with mine?

Surely it would be madness even to try? I had never sailed a yacht single-handed. My longest solo passage in a dinghy was about eight miles. I had sailed to the Azores and back the previous year and seen the wildness of a gale-torn ocean. But there were three of us then. Could I, alone, a woman, hope to survive 4,000 miles of sea, several weeks of solitude?

It was now mid-January. I must not leave Britain later than mid-June if I were to have reasonable weather. I had to give three months' notice to my boss. The decision could not be postponed.

For several days I thought of nothing else. I would find a book unread in my hand. I would sit staring into space. I would go to sleep imagining the difficulties involved, and wake with the thoughts still chasing round my mind.

I could find no good reason for not going. So I decided to go.

2 Preparations

Having made the decision to try the crossing I handed in my resignation from work and got down to planning the project.

The first thing I did was consider what sort of boat to use. The biggest boat I had ever sailed in was twenty-five feet long, and from that experience I reckoned that I would be able to handle a boat thirty feet long but no more. I wanted the longest boat I could handle because the longer a boat is the faster it will travel. I was prepared to spend about £3,500, which meant that my choice was rather limited, for the boat would have to be second-hand and not very new, for that would be too costly. I prepared to cash my assets, but was saved from doing that by an offer from my father to lend me the money, which I gladly accepted.

I looked at the advertisements for boats to see what was available, and consulted Peter Pattinson, in whose boat *Pinta* I had gained my ocean-going experience, mainly on a voyage the previous year to Spain and the Azores. Between us we decided that a Pionier-class boat would be the most suitable. This is a fast cruiser-racer built in fibreglass. The design had been well proved in ocean racing, where boats are really driven hard, so I knew it would be able to stand up to the hammering it would get from the Atlantic.

I set about trying to find a Pionier in good condition. Unfortunately there was a strike of postal and telephone workers at the time and it was difficult to get in touch with people who were advertising their boats in the yachting magazines. However, I had a slice of luck for a chance visit to the Poole Yacht Centre Company led to an appointment to go to the Isle of Wight to see a Pionier which was lying at Cowes.

When I inspected the boat she seemed good. The original varnish inside was still almost perfect and she had a set of new curtains, which showed that someone cared for her. As far as I could tell from a brief examination, the hull and rigging were sound, although there were a few surface cracks in the deck. She seemed to have had little use, for the plastic windows were transparent with little crazing, unusual for a boat eight years old. I liked the look of her and decided to negotiate a price.

After some haggling, her owner, Ric Carpenter, agreed to sell her to me for £3,350, provided that a professional examination was satisfactory to me. The boat was lifted out of the water and examined, and no serious defects were found. The sale was then completed and I became the proud owner of a yacht named *Aziz*. This is an Arabic word meaning 'magnificent' or 'beautiful' and the boat was named after the first owner's favourite polo pony.

She was rather different from the only boat I had owned before. That was an eleven-foot sailing dinghy which I had built in the bedroom of my flat in Bristol three years earlier. *Aziz* was thirty feet long, nearly eight feet wide and weighed about three and a half tons. She was sloop rigged, which means she carried two sails at a time, one in front of the mast and one behind. She had two cabins, the main cabin which had a roof raised above the level of the decks, and leading from that a forward cabin which was under the foredeck and contained two bunks with stowage space underneath. The main cabin was about ten feet long. It contained two seats, one each side, a semi-enclosed lavatory cubicle, a small hanging locker, and a cooking area with a sink and a gas ring. There were a number of lockers for stowing things in, and there was a shelf with cutouts to hold plates and pots. One of the seats was large enough for a man to sleep on. The other was only large enough for a child. There was also a quarter berth, which I intended to sleep in. This was like a tunnel as it extended aft out of the cabin underneath the starboard cockpit seat. It would be difficult to fall out of, even if the boat turned right over.

Aziz had a wardrobe of five headsails, one mainsail and two spinnakers. The headsails, in order of size, were a genoa, which reached up the forestay to the top of the mast and reached back to the middle of the cabin window, a small genoa, a No 1 jib, a No 2 jib, and a storm jib, which reached about a third of the way up the forestay and stretched only a few feet back. I decided to get a No 3 jib, as the difference in size between the No 2 and the storm jib seemed too large.

The mainsail boom was fitted with roller reefing gear for reducing the area of sail presented to the wind. This works rather like a roller blind. You wind a handle and the boom rotates, wrapping the sail around it. The mainsail was also fitted with reefing holes. These are a row of holes parallel to the boom through which a rope can be taken and the sail tied down on itself to reduce the area instead of rolling it round the boom. There were three sets of holes so I could tie in one, two or three reefs, depending on how much less sail I wanted to present to the wind.

The spinnakers were of no use to me, for I had never used one of these brightly-coloured balloon sails, and didn't intend to learn now. These sails are difficult to handle even with a full crew, and I thought I would use twin headsails, one poled out each side, to catch any light winds from astern. Not so efficient, perhaps, but much less likely to cause trouble.

People who have never sailed a boat are often surprised that it is possible to sail towards the direction the wind is coming from. It is all a question of the way the sails are cut and what angle they make to the wind. When the wind is coming from behind the boat the sails are spread out so that the wind will push them, and therefore the boat, along. When the wind is coming from a direction more or less in front of the boat the sails act like an aircraft wing, their curve creating 'lift' which pulls the boat forward. One can get a boat to head about forty-five degrees from the direction the wind is coming from but not closer. The closer one wants to sail to the wind the more nearly fore and aft the sails must be.

While arranging the purchase of *Aziz* I had also been planning the voyage. I decided to leave from Dale, a small village on the fine natural harbour of Milford Haven in south-west Wales, and to aim for Newport, Rhode Island, a well-known American yachting centre.

There were several reasons for choosing Dale as the place to leave from. I had sailed from there with Peter Pattinson on the Azores trip and knew that I would be able to get all the help I needed there. I would not be ignored when I wanted something, as I might be in a larger port. By departing from Dale I would also avoid having to sail down the English Channel, with its vast numbers of ships. I would be a hundred miles north of the Channel, which would give me an advantage when sailing into the prevailing westerly winds of the Atlantic.

At first I had thought of heading for New York, the place all British people think of as the capital city of America. I soon changed my mind when I thought of the problems of entering an unknown and busy port. I would not know where to tie up and I could see myself getting in the way of the big ships. I looked at the chart of the North Atlantic and decided that Newport would be the best place as it is south of Cape Cod, so I wouldn't have to negotiate the difficult waters of the Gulf of Maine.

I decided to leave on Saturday 12 June. This was a compromise between leaving early enough to reduce the chance of encountering a hurricane on the other side of the ocean and leaving me enough time to get ready. There would be six weeks from finishing my job in Cardiff. I determined that before leaving work I would have prepared detailed lists of everything I would need so that I would not be rushing madly around at the last minute.

On Friday 9 April I went to Cowes to collect *Aziz*. The following day Ric, the previous owner, his friend Sue, and I, set off down the Channel on the first stage of the passage round Land's End to Dale. I was glad that Ric could come for he would be able to show me the ropes. I had never been responsible for a yacht. Suddenly *Aziz* looked huge, the sails seemed vast, and the mast seemed to have its head in the clouds.

There was a strong breeze that day and we reached

Weymouth quickly, tying alongside a large yacht for the night Next morning we rounded Portland Bill with very little wind, crossed Lyme Bay and arrived in Torquay, where I reluctantly left *Aziz*.

I was pleased with the way *Aziz* handled on this passage. She seemed responsive to the helm, quite fast and most important, the sails seemed fairly easy to manage. I had been worried that I would find it exhausting raising and lowering them, but it was not such hard work as I had feared it might be.

One disappointment was the self-steering gear that I had had fitted at Cowes. It just did not work, and showed no sign of doing so. The principle of a self-steering gear is that one uses the power of the wind to turn the rudder when the boat is off course. The simplest system one can imagine is to have a vane which is linked to the main rudder in such a way that when the boat changes its heading with respect to the wind the vane turns, activates the rudder, and brings the boat back on the original heading. Such a system only works with a very large vane area. It is more usual to have either an auxiliary rudder much smaller than the main one, or to use a servo blade that harnesses the power of the water, using it to turn the main rudder.

The system I had fitted at Cowes had the vane directly linked to the rudder but did not have the power to turn it. I got in touch with another Pionier owner who had the same gear and he said that his had never worked properly. As I did not have time to fiddle around I decided to cut my losses and get one which was sure to work. I ordered a Hasler Gibbs servo pendulum system, the type used by Francis Chichester in *Gypsy Moth IV*, Alec Rose in *Lively Lady*, and Chay Blyth in *British Steel*. Luckily there was one in stock which was promptly delivered to Torquay. There was no time to fit it there so I stowed the parts away in the forecabin to be taken round to Dale.

I left *Aziz* in Torquay for three weeks until I had finished my job in Cardiff. I went down each weekend and lived aboard, getting used to the gear and doing little jobs such as checking the electric circuits. As I got used to being aboard I became more at ease, as one does with a new car. I was able to move around the deck without tripping over things, and could lay my hands on what I wanted without difficulty. *Aziz* stopped being a stranger and became a friend.

On 1 May I sailed out of Torquay with a friend and headed for the Scilly Isles. These rocky islands mark the western end of the Channel. I planned to stay there for a few days before heading north for Wales. We had a very quiet passage and motored most of the way from the Lizard. About four miles from the islands we inadvertently ran out of petrol. That was when I discovered that one gallon on the tank dipstick meant no fuel for the engine.

We hoisted the biggest sail to catch the tiny breeze and crept towards the hazy shore of St Mary's. As the evening wore on we eased up St Mary's Sound and approached the harbour. The wind died. Out came the dinghy oars. We laboriously paddled over the stern and crept round the rocks. Soon we were offered a tow by a fishing launch, and so entered harbour in a rather inglorious manner. We anchored, tidied up and then rowed ashore for a well-earned drink in the Mermaid bar.

Despite the humiliation of being towed into port I was pleased with the trip. We had arrived in the right place, so my navigation must have been okay. *Aziz* had shown that she would keep moving in the lightest of winds, a very desirable characteristic for I could expect a lot of calm weather around the Azores.

The weather soon changed. I spent six days in the islands being blasted by strong winds. I left for Dale with a fresh south-south-east wind which pushed the boat along well but also made her roll hideously. Both of my crew on this passage were very seasick. Luckily I was not. I did most of the steering during the day, but insisted on having some time off watch in the night. I did not want to approach land without having slept for a day, as fatigue can play hell with one's judgement.

We rolled over the sea at a good speed and sighted land at dawn, before it was obscured by heavy rain. It was a bedraggled crew which finally dropped the anchor off Dale, and rowed hurriedly ashore. I had enjoyed the trip and seen *Aziz* behave well in fresh winds. I think the crew had wished they were dead.

From that time I lived on *Aziz* and worked full time on preparing her for the crossing. The major work to be done was the fitting of the Hasler self-steering gear and the making of boards to cover the windows. These were six feet long and looked vulnerable to breaking seas. I did a lot of small jobs but these two major ones were done by Brian Henshall of the Dale Sailing Company. Brian is an excellent craftsman but will not be hurried. I spent a lot of time biting my fingernails until I discovered that in Pembrokeshire things always get done in the end, and get done well. It is just that there is no appearance of urgency.

I thoroughly enjoyed my weeks in Dale. I was looked after very well by Campbell Reynolds, the owner of the Dale Sailing Company, and his wife Mil, who fed me vast quantities of food and tea and made me feel really at home. Bill Tamsett, the proprietor of the Griffin Inn, was helpful and cheerful, taking telephone messages for me and fending off unwanted callers. Mr and Mrs Rind allowed me the use of their deliciously large bath, in which one is in a world apart. Bunty Cowan, the secretary of the Dale Yacht Club, was very helpful, even to the extent of washing some decidedly nasty sailing clothes. And everyone was ready for a friendly chat.

I planned to sail single-handed to Ireland at the Spring Bank Holiday. I wanted to try out the self-steering gear and myself. Peter Pattinson, in *Pinta*, and John Redfern, in his boat *Sloop John D*, planned to make the crossing as well, so I anticipated a good weekend. *Aziz* was ashore on the trolley and Brian and I worked furiously to finish fitting the self-steering in time to launch on the evening tide. We made it with about forty minutes to spare, and *Aziz* was launched at about 19.30 hours. I motored to a buoy and spent the next hour tidying up and preparing to leave, while Brian spliced an eye into my new anchor warp. At 21.30 hours I hoisted the sails, cast Brian adrift in his dinghy, dropped the mooring, and set off on my first single-handed passage.

As soon as I was clear of the moored boats I latched in the self-steering gear and let go the tiller. Would it work? I watched the wake and to my great delight discovered that it was straighter than it had been when I was steering. I had got a good helmsman aboard.

There was a stout wind and we creamed along, heeled well over. As I tacked past Skokholm Island I caught the edge of the Wild Goose Race, and we crashed into great holes in the sea, sheets of phosphorescent spray flying from the bows. The tide carried us well north and I spent the night hoping that I was not too close to the South Bishop lighthouse, which seemed unpleasantly close.

Eventually I convinced myself that I was not about to run on to the rocks and turned in for a couple of hours' sleep. I woke at dawn and saw some islands to the east, from which I could work out my position.

Aziz was going pretty fast with a strong following wind. In the middle of the morning I sighted a sail ahead. It seemed to be going the same way as me and I guessed that it was *Pinta*. I gradually overhauled her and confirmed my guess. This meant that my navigation was correct, unless Peter was lost, which was not likely as he knows this piece of water very well. I overtook *Pinta* as we both rounded the Conningbeg lightship, and arrived in Dunmore East at about 16.30 hours. I tacked into the harbour to lie alongside *Sloop John D. Pinta* arrived about three-quarters of an hour later and tied alongside *Aziz*. We all went to the yacht club and had a drink, and discussed the crossing.

I had arrived in the right place, at a reasonable speed, and nothing disastrous had happened. The self-steering gear had worked well. I had not worked badly. I had managed the sail changes without enormous difficulty, although I had found it rather exhausting. Probably because I was feeling mildly seasick. I felt confident that I could sail *Aziz* single-handed.

The crews of all three boats ganged up for a splendid meal at the Ocean Hotel. We dressed up for the occasion to prove that one can remain civilized even when living in cramped quarters. The next day was spent idling about the village checking the quality of the local brew. We went out for another good meal in the evening and then rolled back to our respective boats. We changed clothes, hoisted the sails and cast off for the return to Wales.

There was hardly a breath of wind. After a while we all started our engines. I ran mine for about an hour so as to get an offing. Then I switched off. I never had it running again, so had a very slow passage back. I would rather not think about it. I drifted up and down on the tides and took twenty-four hours to cover the last eighteen miles. As in the Scillies I was towed in the final few hundred yards.

I was now quite sure that I could handle the boat. I had ten days left to get everything done. Brian started work on the windows, making some splendid boards with small plastic portholes cut in them. I started the final collection of stores and equipment. It became very hectic. One delightful, but counterproductive, influence was the parties which were given for me. Dale Yacht Club gave me a good do at Sunday lunchtime with the result that I went aboard *Aziz* and spilled a pot of paint over the cockpit floor.

Time rushed by and before I knew what had happened there were only two days left until Saturday 12 June, departure day.

3 Leaving

Only two days left. Things really started moving. I had allowed time to get all the stores on board and stored away on Thursday, before going to Milford Haven dock on the evening tide so that I could complete Customs formalities on Friday.

I had unfortunately not allowed time for talking to Press and broadcasting men. And dozens seemed to turn up, all wanting interviews, all certain that they only needed a couple of minutes, all taking as long as they could get.

Brian was still working on *Aziz*, fitting strengthening battens to the after bulkhead and to the washboards for closing the cabin entrance. I spent the morning getting the food aboard with the assistance of pressganged newsmen. Frankly, I cannot remember exactly what happened that day. I know that I did two television interviews on board. That took up a lot of time. I know that I did some television interviews ashore, for I remember using an anchor as a 'prop', and being delighted to discover that it was one I had ordered but had given up for lost.

Peter Pattinson arrived before lunch bringing a number of plastic water containers for me. Shortly afterwards came Shirley Marsham, who had sailed with me as crew in Peter's boat to the Scilly Isles the previous year. She brought me a splendid selection of Tupperware containers, a welcome present from the makers. These airtight plastic containers make it much easier to keep food dry and tidy.

My parents arrived with Phyllida, my second sister, who had had her leave from her Foreign Office post in the Arabian Gulf put forward so that she could see me off. We had time for a short chat before I was whisked off to do some job. I was sorry not to have more time with them, but arranged to see them in Milford the next day.

I finally escaped from the fuss ashore and went aboard to get ready to take *Aziz* up to Milford. Peter came aboard and Brian decided to carry on working while we moved up the haven. We motored past the oil jetties and dredgers and arrived outside the dock gates just as they were opening, a beautiful piece of timing. A lovely white ketch came out very quickly and shot off up the haven. We cautiously approached the gates, decided that nothing else was coming out and motored slowly in.

I managed to bring *Aziz* alongside a docked lighter without hitting it a terrible thump, despite my hamfisted use of the engine controls. We tied up and climbed over the rubber tyres surrounding the lighter and found that we were only a few minutes' walk from the road entrance. A much better place to be than the corner where yachts usually go, an interminable walk from the entrance round by the fish dock.

We spent a few minutes tidying up and then Peter and I walked up to the Lord Nelson Hotel where he was to stay. I had a bath and changed into shore clothes and after a drink we had a good dinner. Then I walked back to *Aziz*, cleared the junk off my berth and went into a sound sleep.

I woke at about half past seven and walked up to the hotel for the last civilized breakfast I was to have for many a day.

Now the enormity of the whole project hit me. What the hell was I doing? I was going to be alone for an immense time. I might die. I might never see my friends again. I had been so happy the past few weeks doing the things I liked and living among friendly and interesting people. Now it was ended. These weeks had been among the happiest of my life and I was reluctant to give them up, to start a new phase of life, to face the unknown.

But I was still committed to the project so I stiffened my upper lip and got on with it, and with the return to work came the return of confidence and enthusiasm.

When I returned to *Aziz* I was discovered by a photographer who wanted some stills for the BBC. I obliged with poses for a few minutes but then Peter came to say that we could tie along-side a tug exactly opposite the dock entrance. This would be much more convenient for loading stores so we motored round and tied up.

I went up to the Customs House and quickly obtained my clearance papers. Then I went to see the Waterguard, who are responsible for the loading and sealing of duty-free stores. They had not yet got a loading time so I went back to work on *Aziz*.

My parents and Phyllida arrived and produced tins and bags of home-made cakes and biscuits. I had specially requested some of my mother's home-made fruit cake and parkin, a North Country cake made with oatmeal and treacle. The family came aboard and looked at the shambles in the cabin while I wrote a list of the fresh fruit and vegetables that I wanted and various other things which I had forgotten to get. Such as pencil and paper for writing a diary. If I had forgotten those this book would not have been written.

The family went shopping and Peter and I started to stow the stores which were lying higgledy piggledy on the forward berths. This took quite a while, decanting the dry foods into Tupperware and packing the tins in the small well which formed the floor of the forward cabin. I lined this well with the canvas boom cover, which I would not need at sea, so that the tins would not rattle around. It turned out to be an unwise move to use the cover for the tins eventually rusted and stained the canvas.

The rest of the food went on the berths in the forward cabin, much of it in Tupperware and the rest in cardboard boxes or loose. I jammed it tightly together and tied a length of lobster-pot netting over it to hold everything in place. Also in the for-ward cabin went ten gallons of water in clear plastic containers, eight gallons of paraffin in yellow plastic containers, the large anchor, two spinnakers, spare oilskins, camera box, spare battens, spare tiller, anchor buoy, a few books and a roll of charts which should have been left behind as they were for the English Channel.

I was a bit worried that all this weight at the front would make *Aziz* nose heavy, for I only had ten gallons of petrol in the after locker to compensate. However, she seemed all right and I consoled myself with the thought that all my stores would weigh less than a couple of hefty foredeck hands sleeping in the forward berths.

By lunchtime dour rain was pouring from a uniform, grey sky. The family arrived laden with bags of stores and with food for a picnic lunch, and we all crammed into the cabin among the jumble of stores, chandlery and tools. Of course, this had to be the time that the Waterguard came to seal up the bonded stores. It was so wet outside that everyone squeezed into the cabin like sardines in a tin. The bonded stores were checked and the paperwork completed. The spirits and cigarettes were sealed in the locker under the galley which I had rapidly transformed into a bond locker by screwing an eye on to the frame so that string could be taken from the door handle to the eye and sealed with the official lead seal.

My parents did more shopping during the afternoon while Peter, Brian and I carried on working aboard. Brian was working on deck, rigging extra lifelines and strengthening the bracket for the self-steering gear. Peter and I tidied up the cabin using my usual technique of putting everything into lockers and boxes and arranging the boxes neatly on the floor. Peter's boy, Robert, arrived and changed into sailing clothes and soon we were ready to leave the Milford dock and return to Dale.

We motored out of the dock when the gates opened and headed down the haven. We were chased by a motor boat with photographers aboard, so we raised the sails to make a more impressive picture. There was a good breeze accompanying the rain and we went very fast and soon got back to Dale. The wind made it difficult to row to the beach, about half a mile from the mooring, so Peter put me ashore at the nearest point. I climbed up the hill to the road and walked down to the village. It was nice to have a few minutes to myself after the pressures of the day but I could not dawdle as I knew that Phyllida was waiting for me in Dale.

While Phyllida drove me to Haverfordwest I changed from jeans and oilskins to a dress, and looked quite respectable when we arrived at Chez Gilbert, the best restaurant in the area. The family group had expanded to include my third sister, Primrose, and my Uncle Jack and his wife. Unfortunately my eldest sister, Gillian, could not come, for her three children and her husband's medical practice could not be left. We had a good meal, but I was really too tired to appreciate it despite knowing that it was my last meal ashore. I hurried back to Dale, and rowed out to Peter's boat where I was to sleep, *Pinta* being moored much closer to the beach than *Aziz*. I fell quickly into a dreamless sleep.

Next morning I awoke to the realization that the great day had arrived. I was worried that I would not be ready to leave at 11.00 hours which I had published as my departure time. Peter and I fetched *Aziz* from her mooring and anchored her by *Pinta* so that she was as close to shore as possible. I would have to leave on time now or the falling tide would leave the boat aground. Brian turned up in his dinghy and got to work on some final jobs which he thought needed doing to *Aziz*. I rowed ashore to meet the family and to see Bruce Coward, my literary agent, who had brought the contract for this book to be signed. This was important for the non-returnable advance to be paid was almost sufficient to cover the costs of the trip, apart from the boat which was insured. Even if I were forced to give up I would not be in debt.

By the time I had been through the contract clause by clause and signed each page, quite a crowd had gathered. I was delighted to see my friends Jock and Doreen Ferguson, who had been among the first to know of my transatlantic plans. After kisses all round, with my tears bravely held back, I left the beach and rowed back to *Aziz*. I was not to set foot on British soil until two months had passed.

As eleven o'clock approached the water became more and more crowded with boats of all shapes and sizes from rowing dinghies to Campbell's converted lifeboat. They sailed round and round *Aziz* and I felt like the statue of Eros in the centre of Piccadilly Circus. One launch got too close and fouled my anchor warp but fortunately did not unhook us from the bottom. I was getting impatient to go but Brian insisted that we fit the plastic pipes to the spare bilge pump. This involved boiling a kettle of water to soften the pipes. It seemed to take ages to boil but eventually got hot enough and Brian squeezed the pipes on to the pump.

I hurried him into his dinghy, asked Peter and Robert to hoist the sails and at 11.15 hours the anchor was hauled up and we were off.

Peter and Robert stayed aboard to fend off any over-friendly boats. I took the tiller and swung *Aziz* round to head out past Dale Fort to the open sea. There was a stiff breeze from the north-west and I had quite a job trying to sail single-handed without the self-steering latched in, as my hands were full of ropes. I hardly had a moment to watch the escort of boats which followed me weaving to and fro across my wake. The launch carrying a television crew tried to interview me by loudspeaker but I could not understand what was said, besides having *Aziz* and the other boats to attend to. I waved to my family and friends but was really longing to be alone, away from the tensions of the last few days.

As we approached St Ann's Head and the ocean I could see that there was a big swell coming in. I brought *Aziz* head to wind and held her there while Peter and Robert climbed into their rubber dinghy, a perilous operation as the craft bobbed up and down on the swell. I cast off their painter and left them astern to be picked up by the television launch. Then I set the self-steering gear and streamed the log to mark the start of the crossing.

Now I had nothing to do but watch the fleet. One by one they turned back to the shelter of the haven until eventually just *Aziz* and a white yacht were heading out to sea. Finally she too turned back with a parting wave from her crew.

At last, I was alone.

4   First Gale

I wasn't alone after all.

A light aircraft sped over the wave tops and passed immediately above me. I waved. It circled and came over again and continued to make passes over the boat. I guessed that it was taking photographs of me and was rather flattered by such attentions, but I soon got bored with waving and wished that he would go away so that I could be sick in private. I went below and soon he went away. I know now that he was supposed to film my departure with all the boats for television, and that he was heartily cursed for being late.

The weather improved steadily and the sun came out. *Aziz* was going well but I felt rather queasy and was actually sick several times. I wasn't surprised at this as I am always sick first day at sea but after that I never have any trouble, even in the most turbulent seas. But it is unpleasant at the time and I didn't feel like working. I spent some time in my berth and some time in the cockpit, smoking. I have always found that smoking helps me feel less sick though I know that many people do not feel that way. A friend has told me that vile cigars are the thing, but I only had mild cigarettes. Maybe I should have taken tobacco twist to chew like the sailors of old. One trouble about feeling sick when sailing single-handed is that one dare not take a powerful tablet such as Dramamine, as it is so soporific that one cannot react properly. So you have to stick it out.

Apart from the sickness I thought I was feeling quite happy, and wrote in my diary: 'I am feeling remarkably calm after this morning when I had a little cry and wished I wasn't going.' But when I recorded on tape an account of the departure I was

CANADA

Newfoundland

Nova Scotia

Boston

New Haven
New York

Rhode I.

Long I.

quite overcome by emotion. The tape is full of long pauses and choked sentences. I wanted to go back and tell everyone what a marvellous send-off it had been. I wanted to share my emotions with someone else.

I felt rather guilty about letting my parents in for an unpleasant few weeks. They had not let me know their true feelings, as they didn't want to influence my decision, but I knew that they would worry, for what parent wouldn't? I was really much better off than my family and friends for I would always know how I was whereas they would be left to imagine all sorts of ghastly things. They would have no news of me unless I was able to talk to a passing ship, as I was not carrying a radio transmitter apart from a short-range distress radio. If I did die no one would know how or when it happened.

This was my worst fear for those ashore; that I would just not appear, and that eventually they would have to give up hope. Not that I thought I would die. I would not have em-

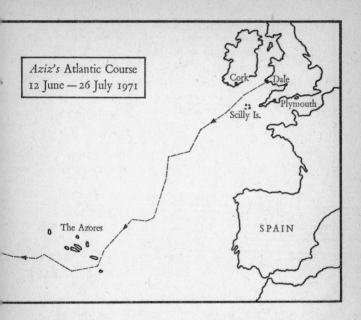

Aziz's Atlantic Course
12 June — 26 July 1971

Cork
Dale
Plymouth
Scilly Is.

The Azores

SPAIN

barked on such a venture unless I thought that the chance of surviving was very good.

As far as I could see there were two possible occurrences which might kill me. One was falling overboard. I frequently had a vision of being in the water watching *Aziz* sailing beautifully over the horizon, the self-steering gear dutifully holding her on course for America. If a boat steered by hand is left unattended she will gradually swing round until the sails are flapping and she stops making way through the water. There is a chance of getting aboard. However, as I can hardly swim, I thought that going overboard would be my funeral in either case. I was not worried about my lack of swimming ability for if I was separated from the boat I would be too far from land for even the best swimmer. I determined to wear a harness with a line that I could clip to the boat for all deck work.

The other possible disaster was being run down by a ship. All vessels are supposed to carry navigation lights and to keep a continuous lookout. I could not carry efficient navigation lights as these require a lot of energy to be visible at a useful range. I could not use electric power as it would have meant running the engine daily, and I could not carry enough fuel for that. I could not use oil lamps as again I could not carry enough fuel.

What I intended doing was displaying a single white light instead of the red and green navigation lights. This light was to come from a Tilley lamp, a gadget which burns vaporized paraffin. It has a tank of paraffin which is vaporized by pre-heating a jet with burning methyl alcohol and pumping air into the tank to create pressure. The vapour burns round a filament like a gas light, and gives an intense white light.

I could not hope to keep an effective lookout in these days of high-speed ships when a ship can be below the horizon only a quarter of an hour before it passes by – or over – you. I decided that I would keep some sort of a lookout when I was in the shipping lanes but otherwise would not bother. After all, the Atlantic is a big place and a ship has to pass within feet to be dangerous, except in heavy weather when a ship's wake can combine with big seas to swamp or capsize a small boat.

I had one safety device: a radar reflector. This is made from three intersecting mutually perpendicular sheets of aluminium, and is designed to reflect radar beams and give a bright spot on a ship's radar scope. If anyone cares to look. I hardly dare complain about poor lookouts, but I believe that many merchant ships do not keep any sort of a watch at sea. Judging by the number of collisions and near misses in the English Channel many ships do not keep an effective watch there. And that is the busiest stretch of water in the world. Why should they bother in mid-ocean?

Apart from these hazards I could not see anything else to stop me surviving. Even if I were dismasted or the rudder fell off or some such thing happened I could call for help on my distress radio. I had an inflatable life raft which was kept in the cockpit ready for immediate use, and I had flares and smoke flares close at hand.

I would, of course, have been reluctant to ask for help, but would do so if it were obviously the only sensible thing to do. People are very good about helping yachtsmen in distress, regardless of inconvenience, but when one undertakes a possibly hazardous voyage one should not rely on help. One must be prepared to live and die unaided and not impose on the goodwill of others.

Whether I would be able to complete the crossing without disturbing my personality was another question. The thought of forty days alone did not appal me, but I was not sure how I would react to being frightened. I did not know whether I would be able to stand frequent frightening circumstances, but was encouraged by the knowledge that a fair number of men have done this or longer crossings without ending up completely insane. In fact, I thought – and still think – that a woman is less likely to crack up than a man. It has often been found that women survive hardship better than men. I think that this is because women are less self-centred than men, for a woman's life is usually centred on her husband and/or children and so she has a motive for fighting on when all is lost. Of course, I could not claim to be in this position, being unencumbered by family responsibilities, but if there is any truth in the argument of evolved innate sex differences, which I think there is, I could expect to have this survival capacity.

It was my first night at sea. The sun sank like a red globe into the water and darkness soon came. As I had seen quite a lot of ships and fishing boats during the day I lit the Tilley lamp and hung it on the boom. It gave a splendid light, completely ruining my night vision so that I had to shade my eyes from the light when looking for other ships' lights. To my annoyance the lamp spluttered and died after about an hour, so I pumped it and relit it, before going below for an hour's sleep. When I came out again I could see the lights of two fishing vessels. Both altered course to pass astern so I felt that the light was doing its job. But shortly after I saw the lights of a big ship heading for me. He did not alter course, and I had to unlatch the self-steering and change course to pass astern of him. I was sure that he had not seen me which was rather worrying.

I slept in short spells because the lamp kept going out. I couldn't find out why, and was a bit depressed at the thought of having to tend it continuously. Later I discovered that it was necessary to fill the tank as full as possible and pump it a lot to get a good pressure in the tank. It was still necessary to flick the on-off knob occasionally to clear the carbon deposit which formed in the jet.

It started raining at 04.00 hours and kept at it until 10.00 hours. Fortunately the wind was from abeam and not astern so the rain did not pour in through the companionway, and I did not have to put in the washboards. I hate being in the cabin with the exit closed as I feel cut off from everything.

At 07.00 hours I changed from the No 1 jib to the No 2 jib as the wind had increased a bit. This was a wet job as green water was coming right over me as the bows dipped into the waves. Despite that, I rather enjoyed it as my new oilskins turned out to be very waterproof, even round the neck where there is usually a leak.

During the morning the wind started to drop and by afternoon I had the maximum sail area raised, full main and big genoa. I spent the day nibbling food, listening to the radio and reorganizing the chaos. I felt rather lonely, as I wanted to tell someone about the trials of the night and the previous day's send-off. To my delight I found a bag with unopened telegrams in it, so I had fun opening them and finding out who had remembered me.

By evening there was very little wind and the sea was smooth. I had noticed that the radar reflector, which was mounted between the starboard lower shrouds, was chafing the mainsail. I decided that as *Aziz* was not rolling much I would haul myself up the mast to the crosstrees and wrap the reflector in rags (so called, really a rather nice tea towel with a green giraffe on it). This was my first experience of going up the mast at sea. I had a block and tackle system specially made for this. The top block was hoisted to the top of the mast on a spare halliard. A line was attached to this block, ran round a ratchet block attached to me, up over the masthead block and down to my hands, so that I had quite a mechanical advantage and could lift my own weight. The lower block was attached to a canvas bosun's chair, once described to me as a 'bottom bra', which I sat in. I could cleat the downhaul line to hold myself in any position and free both hands.

I was able to haul myself up quite easily but rather slowly. As I hadn't dropped the mainsail I couldn't twine my legs around the mast and swung about a bit. I scraped some skin off the inside of my thighs trying to grip the mast with them. I tied the tea towel round the reflector, but it was obviously not a good solution, so I would have to think of something better. Still, it was better than nothing.

After these exertions on deck I went below and amused myself for an hour making a code flag. Each letter of the alphabet is represented by a different flag so that one can communicate between ships. They also each have a special meaning. I was carrying the following flags:

Q – the yellow flag which must be flown on entering a foreign port;

K – 'I wish to communicate with you';

V – 'I require assistance';

U – 'You are running into danger'.

Aziz has a four-letter code – MSOT – which could be flown to identify her. Unfortunately, I hadn't been able to get hold of a T flag and so had to make one.

Fortunately, the T flag is not very complicated to make as it is a tricolour of red, white, and blue. I made it out of a maroon shirt tail, a white petticoat and a blue chiffon scarf. It was, I hoped, recognizable if not beautiful. I rewarded myself with a supper of prawn cocktail, cucumber, tomato and raw carrot. Soon I went to bed.

The wind increased in strength throughout the night and with it the waves rose. At 03.00 hours I was awakened by the sound of pouring rain and got up to change from the genoa to the No 1 jib. I went back to sleep. When I woke at 06.15 hours, *Aziz* was heeled over and slamming her bows on to the waves. I changed to the No 2 jib and rolled the mainsail to the first batten which is about halfway between the first and second sets of reefing holes. At 09.00 hours I took off the jib and put another roll in the main, and at 12.30 hours I rolled the main right up to the second batten, equivalent to just over three reefs. I seemed to spend the whole morning climbing in and out of my oilskins.

The wind was from just east of north and I reckoned that it had reached gale force. The seas were about twelve feet high, the grey of Atlantic warships, with white crests and spume dragging down the backs of the waves. They seemed rather confused, probably because I was over the banks which run up the Irish Sea approaches. *Aziz* was sailing fast on a broad reach with the self-steering just managing to hold her on course. I was rather frightened, for this was the first gale I had been in alone, and the first gale I had been in with *Aziz*. I was not sure how each of us would behave. *Aziz* behaved well, but I have to admit that I spent most of the day in my bunk waiting for the nasty weather to go away.

I couldn't decide whether I should allow *Aziz* to continue her headlong rush or if I should heave to and let her ride the waves gently. I decided to leave her to carry on, mainly because I didn't want to go out on deck to hoist the storm jib. I had to go out in the end as one of the lines from the self-steering to the tiller chafed through. I raised the storm jib, hauled it to windward, pulled the mainsail fairly far in and lashed the tiller about centrally. What happened now was that the jib, being pulled across to the wrong side, was tending to turn the boat away from the wind while the mainsail was trying to turn the boat into the wind. The result was that she lay quietly at about forty-five degrees to the wind, slowly moving forward and drifting sideways. It is remarkable how heaving-to changes the noise and lurching of a headlong rush into the comparative peace of a cork bobbing up and down.

I slept fairly well that night, although I woke frequently to listen to the wind whistling through the rigging wires. At 07.00 hours the whistling had disappeared and I decided that I should start sailing again. I renewed the tiller line, unreefed the main to the first batten and hoisted the No 2 jib. Then I went below to get some breakfast as I was feeling hungry.

I had just wriggled out of the oilskin jacket and was stripping the trousers off when I heard the jib flogging and cracking. I looked out to see what was wrong and found that the sheet had come adrift from the corner of the jib. I hastily dressed again and went to clip it back on again. I didn't want to lower the sail so I grabbed the flapping corner with one hand and the snap shackle on the sheet in the other hand and tried to clip them together. Several times the sail tore itself from my grasp. I was just about to let go the halliard and drop the sail enough to take the wind out of it when I managed to get the clip on. Whew! Quite a fight!

I fried some tomatoes and bread for breakfast and thoroughly enjoyed them. I was glad that I had felt hungry for I had been worried that my appetite had been so small. I was afraid that I would have to force myself to eat.

I wrote in my diary: 'Yesterday has shown me that my re-action to fear is a bad one – I just try to sleep and pretend everything is OK. Must make myself do things.' However I was more confident now that the gale had blown itself out without anything serious happening. The tiller line had chafed through because it was leading round a sharp edge of the self-steering bracket, so I put another block on to keep it clear and give a fair lead.

During the morning I got to work. I started by cutting off the ends of the stainless bolts which Brian had put through the cabin roof and after bulkhead. First I used the little hacksaw but made slow progress so I tried the large hacksaw but couldn't get at the bolts with that. I finally got out my magnificent boltcroppers, a tool rather like an oversized pair of pliers with handles about three feet long. They were rather heavy and like an idiot I dropped them on the steering compass which was mounted on the bulkhead. What a bloody stupid thing to do.

Fortunately, the glass compass top is a hemisphere and therefore very strong, and I only chipped a small hole in it. The liquid in the compass started to run out so I hurriedly got out some flexible sealer and bunged up the hole. I stopped the leak but there was now a rather large air bubble in the liquid. I decided that it would be all right as I could still read the figures and the sealer was on the side away from the steering position and didn't spoil my view of the compass card. I felt very annoyed at myself for being so careless.

Then I did another stupid thing. I had two buckets, one a big farming bucket with a metal handle which I had 'borrowed' from Peter Pattinson, the other a small domestic bucket with a plastic handle. I had a piece of string tied to the handle of the little bucket so that I could throw it over the side and haul in sea water. I threw it over. The sea caught it with a terrific tug and the handle came off. My nice little red bucket floated away astern while I was left holding a piece of string with a handle tied on to it. A ridiculous feeling. But the most maddening aspect was that I knew perfectly well that the handle might come off, for it had happened before. Really, I am getting careless!

At lunchtime I emptied one of the small polythene water bottles which I inherited with *Aziz*. I didn't want it cluttering the boat up so decided to throw it overboard. Then I thought I would send a message in it. But it was no good putting a piece of paper inside for no one would notice it. I really wanted to paint on the outside but hadn't got a suitable brush, so I made do with a chinagraph pencil which gives a waxy mark. I wrote my name, the boat's name, the date, my course and my log reading, and addressed it to Peter Pattinson. It should have drifted up the Channel or the Irish Sea. It has not been reported, but I didn't expect it to be. It was just a bit of fun for I liked the idea of sending a message in a bottle.

The wind carried on moderating and by the afternoon I had the full main and No 1 jib up. I managed to get a decent noon sight which put me 250 miles from Dale, not bad going. After my efforts of the morning I took the afternoon off and idled about reading *The Nun's Story* and pottering around.

My appetite was improving and when I came across a packet labelled in my mother's writing 'Honey cake. Eat first' I obeyed the instruction immediately and ate the lot with a cup of china tea with a slice of lemon in it. By evening I was hungry again and made myself a large macaroni bolognese. I ate it all and promptly felt immensely sleepy. So I went to bed.

5 Snags

The weather was peaceful that night so I had nothing to do except periodically pump up the Tilley lamp. I slept well apart from these excursions, and finally woke at about o8.oo hours. Half an hour later a line of black cloud passed over bringing a short burst of wind which sent *Aziz* scuttling over the sea. It was soon over and we continued to potter quietly onwards.

I felt pretty rotten, though, as if I had a hangover. This wasn't very likely as, for once in my life, I hadn't had a drink for days. Perhaps it was a reaction to sobriety; my body adapting itself to running on pure blood instead of the usual blood-alcohol mixture!

But it felt like flu. I took a couple of aspirin and huddled up in my sleeping bag feeling sorry for myself. I felt miserable all day and kept taking aspirin and then going back to sleep for a while. During the afternoon I started to ache all over and this convinced me that I really did have flu and was not imagining things.

The night was decidedly unpleasant. I kept waking in a sweat and throwing back the sleeping bag to cool off. Then I would get cold and huddling up again would go back to sleep, to dream furiously before waking again in a sweat. Fortunately, we were all but becalmed throughout the night so there was no need for me to work the ship at all apart from checking the tell-tale compass above my head to see that we were on course. Actually this involved rather more mental effort than you might think. Because the compass was mounted close to various metal instruments the reading was about thirty degrees in error, so I had to work out what the course really was. Sometimes I would do my calculations wrong and scramble out of bed into the cockpit to look at the steering compass only to find that we were on course after all. I never discovered if the opposite happened: me thinking that *Aziz* was on course when really she was heading in the wrong direction. I expect it did.

I did nothing to help the boat that night for it did not seem necessary. Indeed, I doubt whether I could have forced my body out on deck and made it work unless there had been a real panic when I would probably have forgotten about feeling ill. I find that when I am ill my mind and body become more differentiated. Usually I am not particularly aware of being a mind-body union. Even when there is a difference of opinion between the parts, such as when one has a blister but wants to walk, it is the union which decides. However, when ill, or drunk, or under stress, the union breaks down and the constituents hold public discussion and decide the issue by a trial of strength.

The character of the whole is determined by the balance struck between the parts. When conditions change so that different stresses are imposed the balance is altered and the character is changed. This was one of the things I was trying to find out about myself. Simply, when conditions were seriously threatening the physical part how would the whole react? Would there be disintegration of the union and if so how would the mental part compensate? Would it be able to accept reality, or would it retreat into a world of dreams where the body could no longer overload the mind with unacceptable messages.

One of the possible stresses was illness. When planning the voyage I tried to find out what medical emergencies might arise. It seemed to me that one could divide the possible sources of illness into two types.

The first type would be due to infection, probably by bacteria or viruses already present in or on the body. Such illnesses as bronchitis, pneumonia and chronic diarrhoea were possibilities. These would require treatment by drugs.

The second type would be due to physical violence. One expects to suffer minor injuries such as cuts, abrasions, bruises, torn nails, and must be prepared to put up with them. One does not want a serious injury. One could break a bone by falling or getting in the way of moving gear. One could have fingers or toes crushed by being trapped by moving ropes or pinched between moving parts of the boat. One could get severe rope burns or burns from cooking accidents. One could be concussed by being struck on the head by the boom.

I asked my brother-in-law, Geoff, for advice on a medical kit and he provided me with a collection of drugs and instructions on their use. They were mainly antibiotics in various forms, and pain killers, mild and strong. I also had some anti-sleep pills for those occasions when it would be necessary to stay awake. I had a first-aid kit packed in a shoe box. This contained bandages, burn dressings, plaster bandages for setting fractures, local anaesthetic ampoules and syringes, and needles and thread for stitching wounds. I also had a roll of gauze which had come from my grandfather's surgery. He stopped practising medicine well over fifty years ago, but the roll was still in its original wrapper. Along with my old sextant it was the oldest thing on the boat.

As well as these emergency supplies I had some vitamin and trace element pills which I took intermittently. I didn't expect to show signs of vitamin deficiency even without them, as it takes about six weeks for the symptoms to show. My food supply contained a fair supply of everything, but I occasionally took pills just in case.

Several people asked me why I didn't have my appendix removed, and if I wasn't worried about getting appendicitis. I have never understood why this should be such a common fear. Why should my appendix start complaining now, after twenty-eight years without trouble? Surely the chances of dying of appendicitis on this trip were not materially different from the chance of dying on the operating table having it out as a precautionary measure. Pretty small. If I did have trouble I had sufficient antibiotics to control the inflammation until a ship responded to a distress signal.

The next morning, Day 6, I got up at 07.00 hours because I had backache from lying down for so long. It was a beautiful morning; sunny, with a few clouds and a crawling silver sea with a long Atlantic swell. There was a perfect breeze from the south-west and *Aziz* kept up a comfortable five knots. The horizon was very clear and I got a good sextant sight in the morning and another at noon to fix my position. For the first time I was east of the desired track to the Azores. This was because I had been on the southern tack most of the previous day.

The system used to find one's position from the sun is as follows. Using a sextant you measure the angle between the sun, yourself and the horizon. This is known as the altitude of the sun. If you know the time precisely and your position roughly it is a simple matter to work out from tables the position of an imaginary line, the position line, at right angles to the sun's bearing from you, on which you are placed somewhere. By taking sights at different times of the day, when the sun's bearings are different, you can get two position lines, and where they cross is your precise position. Of course one has to allow for the distance travelled between taking the two sights.

The way I tried to work my sights was to take one in the morning, when the sun was due east, from which I would get a position line which was my longitude. At noon, when the sun was due south, I would take another sight which would give me my latitude. I would plot these lines on the chart and move the longitude forward the distance I reckoned I had travelled. This gave me my position at noon.

Sometimes, of course, the sun would not be visible at the appropriate time. Then I would take sights when I could and cross the position lines for a fix, and from that work back or forward to a noon position.

All this was great fun, and I always looked forward to doing my daily navigation. Occasionally I would take sights of the moon or planets, not because it was necessary but because they were so beautiful that it seemed a shame not to use them.

I was not feeling as bad as the day before, but was still head-achey. I did not have a proper meal but ate snacks all day and sorrowfully contemplated the bond locker with all the booze and cigarettes in it, regretting that so far I hadn't felt like any debauchery.

I spent most of the day reading *The Elizabethan Epic* by Lacey Baldwin Smith. It was interesting but I found that it was not detailed enough. Maybe I was too ignorant of the period to appreciate the background.

The interior of the boat was still rather a shambles. I hadn't yet been able to get into the heads, or toilet compartment, as the swing of the door was stopped by all the boxes on the cabin floor. It didn't worry me very much as I went over the side of the boat instead, which is just as good and really less trouble as you don't have to pump water in and out of the bowl. In fact, I never used the heads for the proper purpose.

I noted that it was about time I got the floorboards up and pumped the bilge out. This would have to wait until I had reorganized the chaos on top of the boards somewhat. I didn't feel up to doing that.

During the afternoon I passed through a patch of fragmented foam. I don't know what it was but imagine that it was some sort of pollution from a ship. I'm afraid that my own contribution to ocean pollution was rather greater than it might have been. I tried to make sure that all cans and bottles sank immediately, but was careless with polythene. Ideally I should have kept it all for destruction on land, but I just threw it all over. One is not encouraged to make a great effort to keep half a dozen containers when one knows that the ocean liners discharge all their waste into the sea.

In fact, I saw very little evidence of pollution. I had only two small lumps of oil come aboard, though the mess they made was quite disproportionate to their size. I saw one or two floating bottles and an occasional small piece of wood. On the return from the Azores last year we had seen quite a lot of light bulbs floating past, Lord knows why. This time I didn't see any.

At some time during the day I crossed the track we had made last year from the Azores to the Scilly Isles. We had had a most frustrating passage with long periods of calm. But in this area we had been overtaken by a Force 9 gale. The waves had been long and high with breaking crests. We were frequently washed by waves and one broke into the heavily-reefed mainsail ripping it from side to side. The wind blew at gale force for over a day and we drifted about sixty miles due east. We were lucky to have plenty of sea room for many unfortunate craft in British and French coastal waters were damaged and some foundered, trying to keep off the shore.

Before retiring to bed again that evening with a couple of aspirin I took off the genoa and put on the No 1 jib, for the wind had strengthened a little. I put about on to the port tack making a course due west.

My procedure for changing foresails was then as follows:

1. Dress up in oilskin jacket and trousers and safety harness;
2. Get new sail and old bag out of after locker (the large locker with a round hatch behind the cockpit);
3. On to foredeck to tie bags to pulpit;
4. Back to cockpit to slacken off sheet;
5. To mast to uncleat halliard;
6. To bows holding halliard to catch sail as it drops;
7. Unhank and bag old sail;
8. Unbag and hank on new sail;
9. Clip on sheets and halliard;
10. Hoist new sail and cleat halliard;
11. To cockpit to tighten sheet;
12. To mast with winch handle to winch halliard taut and stow halliard tail;
13. Fetch sailbags from foredeck and stow in after locker;
14. Adjust sheet as necessary;
15. Adjust self-steering as necessary.

The great majority of these sail changes could be made without altering the setting of the self-steering gear. *Aziz* was sufficiently responsive and the self-steering sufficiently powerful for a course to be held even when the sails were grossly unbalanced. This was a great advantage, for I found that in heavy weather *Aziz* would sail most courses with only a jib or with only a main.

The above procedure sounds rather complicated but was in fact quite simple unless I inadvertently left out a step. This could be a terrible nuisance as I would probably have to go back to an earlier stage. I suppose it took about twenty minutes to start with, but soon I could do it much faster if the conditions weren't too bad. Wearing a safety harness slowed me down as I had to unclip and reclip the harness line three times to get from the cockpit to the bows. Sometimes I would trip over the line or get it wound round something. But I had promised my mother that I would wear it, so I did. I never wore a life jacket because I was afraid that if I did fall in it would be a handicap in those few moments when I might be able to get back on board. If I didn't get back and was left floating in the ocean I wanted to drown quickly rather than slowly for there would be no chance of surviving.

After changing the sail I lit the Tilley lamp and stood it on the step over the engine so that I could read by its light. And the inevitable happened: I knocked it off. The glass globe shattered on the floor, the mantle broke and a jet of hot paraffin sprayed all over the place. I grabbed the thing, turned off the paraffin and burned myself on the vaporizer. I dropped it again and cursed heartily. After regaining my composure I found the rubber-covered torch and by its light picked up the fragments of glass and threw them overboard. Then I wiped up the spilt paraffin as best I could and wedged the lamp on the floor.

Well, I had solved the problem of keeping the lamp showing outside all night. I couldn't, for without the glass the lamp would only burn in still air. I would just have to keep my fingers crossed and hope that I didn't get run down. Actually it was rather a relief, for I would be able to sleep more peacefully, not having to get up and pump the lamp at intervals. Fortunately, I was well clear of the shipping lanes.

It was a beautiful night and without the lamp alight I could really see the milky phosphorescence. If I put my head over the side and looked back along the wake it seemed like a runway rushing away, while from standing height it looked like a comet trail. I love phosphorescence and could spend hours hypnotized by the little lights rushing by.

The following morning, Day 7, I felt very much better and hardly had a headache. I looked at my watch to see what time it was, and found that it had stopped. The inside of the glass was misted over so I suppose that water had seeped in. I was a bit upset because it had been reliable and had been easy to read. I had bought it the previous year at Beirut Airport and it had served me faithfully and waterproofly throughout the Azores trip. I didn't have another watch but had a travelling alarm clock, a tin alarm clock and the navigation chronometer, so was not worried about not knowing the time.

During the morning I arranged the boxes on the floor and pumped the bilge. The bilge pump was fitted in a stupid place, inside the heads compartment. I had to lift the floorboards, open the exit cock of the toilet and put the exit pipe from the pump into the toilet bowl. I then worked the pump, which transferred water from the bilge to the bowl, from which it is supposed to run into the sea by gravity. This is all right when the boat is on an even keel or heeling to starboard, but when she is heeling to port the water will not run out and one must pump out the toilet as well. Not quite the system for an emergency. I was, however, carrying a portable gusher pump which I kept in the after locker.

This time I had no trouble and got rid of quite a lot of murky water. This was a good thing as *Aziz* had bounced about in the night and the bilge water had made the bottoms of several boxes rather soggy.

I also rigged an aerial for the radio by taking a wire on to one of the bolts from the mast step through the deck. It was difficult to get a good contact as there wasn't enough of the bolt showing for me to wrap the wire round it. I could only stick it on with insulating tape. Nevertheless, reception was vastly improved so I assumed that the mast was acting as an aerial. I could pick up BBC Radio 2 again and get the shipping forecasts, which were useful for the general synopsis of weather although I was now out of the forecast areas.

The wind started to rise and for the first time I hoisted my new No 3 jib, the smallest sail apart from the storm jib. It was really a working jib for a Folkboat, a twenty-five-foot yacht, and was not quite the right shape for the Pionier as it needed the sheet taking farther forward than I could manage, to get the pull in the right direction. The solution was to raise the whole sail farther up the forestay by putting an eighteen-inch strop between the foot of the sail and the deck. I resolved to do this when I had time, but left the sail as it was for the time being.

This new jib had a very nice shape and showed up the other sails which were rather baggy from use. I think I should have bought more new sails as I am sure I would have made better speed with flatter sails. I shall know better next time.

Next time?

'Day 8, 07.30 hours. Have just got up to put about onto the port tack for a change. Now everything will gradually slide to the other side of the boat. Slept well last night but had vivid dreams of going to a big dinner party at a Berni-ish place which I knew was in Bristol, and having huge pieces of red beef cut by a mountaineer. At the time I thought I had done a clever re-materializing act because I knew *Aziz* was out here on the ocean. A second dream was of arriving at a hotel from off the boat with my parents, and being given some letters and a first-class meal, but the most impressive thing was that they had three toilets all in one huge bathroom! I'm afraid I'm going potty after all!'

I had a lot of vivid dreams while on *Aziz* and can remember quite a number of them. I usually dream a lot and thoroughly enjoy myself. I wonder if this is a necessary quality for staying happy when alone, for one gets stimulation from these dreams which is a substitute for external stimulation.

The sky and sea were both a steely grey and *Aziz* was going well with small sails. I heard on the radio that the Navy had had a sad day. A sailing race from Plymouth to Fowey had been hit by a sudden gale and the boats scattered. Two men died and ten were in hospital. It must have been very unpleasant.

I got very worried about my navigation. I took three sights in the morning and the answer they gave seemed a long way out. After checking my calculations and trying to work out what could be wrong I concluded that the sextant must be giving erroneous readings. I started by checking the index error. This is the difference between the angle of the sun above the horizon as read off the sextant and the true angle. I checked it by looking at the horizon and lining up the reflected image with the real image. If there was no error the sextant should read 0° 00'. It is usual to have an error of about 0° 05' due to the mirrors being slightly out of parallel. Mine had an error of 0° 40'! And I had been assuming an error of 0° 06'. One minute of arc equals one nautical mile so my positions were about thirty-five miles out. No wonder they didn't match up very well.

I reset the sextant by adjusting the angle of the mirror. At noon I took sights with that sextant and with an old one which I had as well. This was a most attractive instrument but had a brass scale inlaid with silver and a vernier scale for fine measurement and was extremely difficult to read, although it gave a much better image of the sun. The two instruments agreed and I breathed a sigh of relief. I was still averaging over a hundred miles a day on the log, which is about four and a quarter knots, so I was quite satisfied with my progress. Nevertheless I was still a bit depressed about the navigation as I wasn't sure that the sextant was the only problem.

Then, to lift my spirits, I saw my first shearwater.

6 Sailing through the Spout

One of the pleasures of ocean voyaging is the enjoyment of natural things. There is more life about the surface of the seas than you might think. From the smallest plankton, visible only when it lights up with fear, to the great whales the presence of life is evident.

The most common birds in the mid-Atlantic are petrels and shearwaters. Petrels are delightful little birds, dark brown with a flash of white above the forked tail. They flit to and fro across the waves, continually changing direction, searching for specks of food on the surface. Their feet hang down and the birds look as though they are dancing on the water. This is why they are called petrels, for St Peter walked on the sea. In a mirror calm you can sometimes see the ripples when they touch the surface. In a howling gale you still see them, flying a few inches above the water, dodging the seas with amazing skill, rising above the crests to flit again into the hollows. My spirits were lifted when I watched their joyful dance.

The shearwater is a less delicate bird. A greenish brown on top with a white underside, he curves and swoops in graceful swings from wave to wave. Like a gull following a plough he searches the turbulent wake for scraps of food.

I spent a lot of time watching these birds, and regretted that I hadn't a camera good enough to record their beauty.

Although I am less than a third of the way across I pick up an American show on the short-wave radio. It is a sort of 'In Town Tonight' for New York, in which visitors to the city are interviewed. It seems a world away from *Aziz*, but I am sorry when it is ended, to be followed by dull pop music.

I start to wonder if I am changed in any way by being alone for a week. I feel the same; no happier, no more frightened, no more lonely. I do want to talk to someone and tell what has happened in the time since I left Dale, but do not feel distress because I cannot so do. The radio is a great help as it keeps me in touch with reality.

I listened mainly to talk programmes as there was not much music broadcast on the short-wave bands, and when there was some music reception was not good enough to make it worth listening to. But I enjoyed current affairs programmes, news, discussions, and plays, not to mention commentaries on cricket, rugby and tennis matches.

It is encouraging to hear an American programme. It makes me feel that I am going somewhere, not just sailing into the unknown. I imagine what the seamen on Columbus' ships must have felt. They must have been terrified as they kept sailing towards the rim of the world, wondering what happened when you reached it. Would you fall off into oblivion? I bet the lookouts were on the ball.

But suppose I never see a ship nor any sign of an outside world? Will I mind? Do I miss human company? I think of the periods in my life when I have been far lonelier than I am now. For then I was lonely among people. Now I am alone by myself.

My first recollection of loneliness is of my years at boarding school. When I first went at the age of eleven I was very happy, full of confidence and looking forward to a new experience. After two weeks I was put up a class into one where I was the youngest. Some of the older girls were very unkind to me. No doubt they resented this new girl who was brighter than them. I was astonished. No one had ever treated me like this and I was completely unequipped to deal with such a situation. So I withdrew into myself and became a very solitary person, grateful when I was included in a group but without the courage to make the first approach.

I gradually modified this attitude as I grew older with people I knew, but it returned when I went to university. The difference here was that I soon had a boyfriend and did not have to make my own friends, for we did everything together. But after a year my confidence grew and I dared express opinions of my own. Eventually we parted, and I went through the worst period of loneliness I have ever experienced. I knew practically nobody apart from mutual friends, and with those people I did know I was too proud to admit my loneliness outright and ask for company. I was still frightened of being rebuffed.

But then it dawned on me that I had been too inward looking and hadn't considered that other people might be the same as me. I realized that if you are friendly to people they are likely to be friendly in return. But you can't expect them to make the first move and you must respond clearly to any move that is made. It worked wonders. Since then I have had much less difficulty with personal relationships and have had no long bouts of loneliness and despair.

Even so, I had acquired the habit of solitude and cannot do without it. I get very wrought up if I cannot have time alone. So I was not appalled by the thought of being alone.

I thought of the future.

'It is a funny thing to think of a future which may not exist and, if it does, is ill defined. For example, I don't know what tomorrow will hold for me – will it be another grey day with no sun and no excitement, or will it be a heavenly day or will it be a fearful day? And if fearful, man-made or nature-made fears?'

It was a very curious feeling. This was the first time I had been really aware of the non-existence of the future. Until a happening happens it does not exist. One can imagine that it exists in the future but this is a mere technique of thinking, reflected in our language, just as imaginary numbers are only a technique of calculation. It is, of course, possible to construct an image of tomorrow, store it in the mind and compare it with reality when tomorrow is now. Most people have sufficiently well-ordered lives to obtain a good match. But isn't it fun when something unforeseeable occurs? Isn't this the real pleasure of living? If it were not so one could exist entirely in one's mind, never looking out at the world and never taking in new ideas from other minds. Perhaps some people can do this. I can't. I need stimulation from other people.

So we come back to loneliness. Why did I think that I could face six weeks without interaction with the world of people? Because I planned it, I expected it and I expected it to end. I would not be lonely, for that is a state in which you wish for a relationship with some person. I had relationships which I knew were continuing. I was thinking of my friends and I knew they were thinking of me. But if I were flung into isolation without preparation and without hope I would be lonely, and despair. To be taken from life and thrown into prison without hope of release would be appalling. But to be in mid-Atlantic in my own boat with books, radio, food and drink, through my own choice, is rather enjoyable. So long as nothing goes wrong.

I had now settled to a pattern of eating which rather amused me. I had always maintained that the human body is badly designed with regard to fuel requirements. It would be much better to eat only once every two days, and then do it really well so as to satisfy the aesthetic side without being surfeited. Surely this is far preferable to eating ordinary food every few hours just to satisfy one's energy requirements? The odd thing was that now I had complete freedom to eat as I wished I spent much of the day nibbling away at little bits of this and that. I think this must be because I had so little to occupy myself with that food became a major source of experience.

In the morning I would have a bowl of muesli, a mixture of oatmeal, cereal, nuts, raisins and apple flakes. You add milk and the mixture swells to make a nourishing and filling meal. I was using Ever Ready milk, which is heat-treated so that it will last, unopened, for months. My cartons were dated for use by 11 November 1971, so I didn't expect to have trouble with it going sour. Its only disadvantage is that it tastes foul in tea, but otherwise it tastes all right.

During the morning I would probably eat some fruit, an apple while they lasted, or a carrot or an orange. I might well have some cheese or some of my mother's home-made biscuits.

Around noon I would have a tin of prawns, sardines or spam, or perhaps an egg with mayonnaise, followed by cheese or fruit and a can of beer. At teatime I would have a mug of China tea with a slice of lemon accompanied by a considerable number of biscuits or a few slices of cake.

In the evening I would have a hot meal of some sort. Macaroni bolognese *à la Aziz* was a favourite. I made this by slicing and frying an onion, adding a tin of mince and stirring it around for a minute or two, then adding a little water, a fair bit of tomato paste, a bay leaf, salt and pepper and a handful of quick macaroni. Simmer for twenty minutes and you have a tasty dish. Because my onions were large and my tins of mince full size I always ended up with vast quantities. I would usually have to give some to the fishes but sometimes I would wade through the lot and then fall back in a stupor. I never got bored with food for I had a good variety on board. I had such vast quantities that I only ate the things I really liked, and didn't have to face the unappetizing things like stewed steak.

Cooking was usually quite easy, even when the weather was rough, because the gas burner was pivoted so that it would remain horizontal as the boat rolled. Next to the burner was a sink which I used as temporary storage for implements which were in use but not immediately required. I did not use it for washing as it was easier to use a bucket in the cockpit. All dirty dishes and cutlery were put in the bucket and when I felt inclined I washed them with sea water and liquid detergent. I washed myself in the same way, in sea water. I did not want to waste any of my forty gallons of fresh water and once you start washing in it the precious fluid soon vanishes.

All the food was stowed in the forward cabin, except for immediate use supplies which were behind the galley. On the evening of the ninth day I was getting a tin from the collection in the central well when I noticed that there was a pool of blue liquid in each of the side wells. I smelt it and discovered that it was paraffin which must have leaked from the yellow cans. Nothing seemed to be damaged except two books which had somehow got mixed in with the stores, so I fished out the paraffin cans and put them in the cockpit before mopping up the mess with a sponge and bucket.

When I examined the cans I found that they were not holed but that the leak was from the caps. The rubber washers had swollen and were rumpled up inside the cap. I decided to cut them to size and had just got out the scissors when I was surprised by a noise.

'Hshwhewou!' Like an engine letting off steam.

'What the devil's that?' It was like the sound of dolphins' breathing vastly magnified. It must be a whale.

I leapt up smartly and looked about. Despite the settling dusk I could see a smooth patch of sea gently seething a hundred yards away from the port bow. Then came another 'Hshwhewou' from the other side. I jerked my head round and saw a spout of mist hanging above a shiny dark back which sank slowly beneath the water. Then I heard an even louder blow, and the first whale rolled out of the sea a mere fifty feet from *Aziz*. My heart thumped for this was just too close. 'Mind my boat.' I imagined the thump, the dreadful lurching, the snapping of the rigging, the gushing of the water over me as one of these huge beasts surfaced under me. 'For Christ's sake, mind me.'

The second whale surfaced and blew a little farther away, followed by the first a few hundred yards to my left. And again, to right and left of me, then in front, like great dolphins. 'Thank heavens, they do know I'm here!' My agitation subsided and I settled down to watch the show. First I would hear the blow and, looking round, would see the spout rising fifteen feet or more into the air and gradually disperse downwind. A long, long muddy brown back would roll under the spout and eventually a fin would break the surface. Then the creature would gently sink away leaving a smooth eddying patch of water to mark its excursion. I never saw head nor tail, but the visible part must have been over thirty feet long so I guessed that the total would be over fifty feet. The weight would therefore be between fifty and seventy-five tons, compared with *Aziz*'s three and a half tons.

I sailed through the spout of one. This is the exhaled breath and I had read that it smells particularly fetid. This hardly smelled àt all, just a warm moist air. I noticed bits of red-orange stuff floating in the blow patch, but could not imagine what this could be.

I think these must have been sperm whales. That is the type they catch in the Azores, harpooning them by hand from open boats, a heroic but bloody business.

After the pleasure my whales had given me I didn't want them to end up that way.

I shouted, 'Keep clear of the Azores. Good hunting!'

7 A Thousand Miles Away

The next morning, Day 10, I was worried again about my navigation. I took a number of sights which did not agree very well. The general opinion was that I was east of my last position, which was a very odd result since I had been making a course well to the west of south, and the current was not supposed to be at all strong. I should have worked out a dead reckoning position but stupidly didn't, mainly because I had left behind the graph paper on which to draw the distance run on each course since the previous fix. Even so, I could recognize a stupid answer when I got one.

I sat down in a huff and started to read one of my navigation books to see if I could get an idea of what had gone wrong. Suddenly it dawned on me that it is possible to use the Consol position fixing system without having the special Consol charts, if you have the appropriate Admiralty List of Radio Signals, which is Volume 5.

Consol is a system designed for aircraft navigation and is not very accurate, but one would expect to be within twenty miles which was good enough for me. It works like this: each Consol transmitting station – there are five in Europe – sends out a radio signal which consists of a number of dots followed by a number of dashes, or vice versa. The number of dots and dashes – the total is always sixty – depends on the observer's bearing from the transmitter. All you have to do is count the dots or dashes and look up the tables which give a number of dots or dashes against bearing. If you use two or three stations you get bearings which you can cross for a position. Easy!

I got the radio tuned in pretty smartly and picked up Ploneis, which is in Brittany, and Lugo, which is in northern Spain.

The signals were rather faint as I was at extreme range and I had difficulty counting the dots. However I managed to reach the same figure on several counts, and duly worked out a position. This turned out to be rather farther north than I thought I was. Oh dear.

At noon I got a meridian altitude which gave me a position about a hundred miles south of the Consol fix. This seemed more likely and in the afternoon I got another sight which when crossed with the noon sight, suitably adjusted for course and distance run sinee noon, gave a position which I was happy to believe, though I wasn't a hundred per cent convinced.

I did quite a bit of writing in my diary.

'13.15 hours. I am sitting here smoking and drinking brandy and smelling gorgeous, as I have just daubed myself with scent to cheer myself up. I think that living on this boat is like moving into a new flat. For the first week or so one hasn't enough to do apart from look after the place, but after a while one settles down and is able to while away the hours doing very little. *Aziz* is doing well and I am a bit ashamed of the chaos inside, but by now it is a more organized chaos and I know where to find everything (I think).'

You will have gathered that I am not an obsessively tidy person but am happy if my chaos is organized and I know where everything is. The cabin would have offended many sailors because it was apparently a shambles. In fact, it was quite logically stowed for one person. There were boxes on the floor containing carbonated drink, fruit, chandlery and cordage, there was a large tin containing home-made cake and there was the spare battery which made a useful coffee table. Also on the floor were the permanently damp things, safety harness and oilskin jacket and trousers.

Under the table which bridges the settee was the equipment which was in frequent use or might be needed quickly: the signal lamp, the distress radio, the loudhailer, the cameras and my spectacles, all jammed tight with books and my handbag. Jeans and towels hung over the heads door and a sweater huddled in the corner of the settee. I can just see the expression on the face of many a proud boat owner.

The area behind the gas ring and sink was choc-a-bloc with packets and bottles of pickles, herbs, spices, curry powder, instant coffee, tea, mayonnaise, cooking oil, vinegar, salt, pepper, mustard, vitamin pills, lemon juice, sugar, rice, oat-meal, muesli, orange squash, whisky and brandy. And other things. All was packed solid so that it would not rattle about. On a shelf above were mugs, bowls and more food containers. In the locker beneath were pans, bottles of spirits, cigarettes, and bottles of methyl alcohol for starting the Tilley lamp.

It would have been impossible for a stranger but this chaos was my chaos, created with my own hands, and I liked it.

I did not have the luxury of a chart table and did all my plotting with the chart on the windward settee, kneeling on the floor or sitting on the cake tin. It was difficult at times to keep my balance when *Aziz* was pounding to windward and so the accuracy of my plotting was not up to ocean-racing standards. However, I was not trying to be within two or three miles, but would be satisfied to be within ten miles and not unduly worried if I were twenty miles out.

'I feel that I should be developing some grand philosophy of life, being all alone with plenty of time to think. But I don't feel any different, or more inclined to soul searching than usual. Of course, with a basically humanistic, hedonistic philosophy like mine I don't feel any real guilt and therefore no necessity for justification. In spite of being alone with the natural elements I do not feel closer to a personal god. Rather I feel that I am another piece of flotsam (or jetsam) subject to natural forces. Only when I am frightened do I think of a personal deity and that is (*a*) human and (*b*) cheating. One must live by one's beliefs and involve God equally when happy and when frightened. I must say that natural beauty gives me a sense of gratitude to the Creator – who I do believe in.'

This is a fair statement of my beliefs. When I was in my late teens and early twenties I counted myself a Christian, read books about Christianity, went to church, gave my tithe to the collection and tried to behave as a Christian ought. It made me feel rather miserable because much of the time I could not honestly feel that I needed forgiveness: even when I had done something which I knew was wrong I could not truly ask to be forgiven. I knew that if the same circumstances arose again I would behave in a similar manner. In other words I suffered from guilt; not the guilt of having done wrong but the guilt of knowing I must be doing wrong – no man is perfect – and not believing it.

I eventually gave up trying to be a Christian because I knew that my behaviour would remain the same but that I would be happier without this guilt about not feeling guilty.

So why is it that when danger threatened I called on God for help, a god who I do not believe in, for my god is an observer of people not a participant in human affairs. The call is forced out in desperation, to relieve the mind of the strain of keeping the whole person in balance. It is not made in a religious spirit, with faith that it might be effective. So when I say I prayed I am misleading you. I know what prayer should be, and my cries did not resemble prayer in any meaningful way.

Since ceasing to call myself a Christian I have had much more peace of mind. I have worked out a system of living which involves doing exactly what I want to do. This is actually quite difficult for I have to decide what I really want to do deep down and the consequences of such an action, the possible hurt to other people and therefore to me. To make a decision on this basis requires considerable analysis of these consequences and is excellent exercise for the mind. But when I can reach no clear resolution of a conflict I make a decision on an emotional basis. The most foolproof method I have discovered for doing this is to toss a coin, but instead of abiding by the fall of the coin I note my reaction to the choice it has made and can thus determine which alternative I really want to follow.

It is in working out the consequences of an action that conscience comes in. It is conscience that stops us all being selfish, grabbing, inconsiderate barbarians. Conscience is the learned set of values of a culture which enables people to live together in reasonable harmony. It is the civilizing factor. And, man being what he is, there is not only absence of guilt but also positive pleasure in obeying the strictures of conscience, since mental tension within and, frequently, between people is reduced.

It is therefore essential that children be taught the values of the society into which they are born so that when they become pleasure-seeking adults instead of pain-avoiding children they will still be able to maintain naturally an overtly unselfish mode of behaviour. Indeed some of their pleasure will be derived from this sociable pattern of behaving, although much will be independent of it. But unless they know the values of society how can they question them constructively?

I had fun filling the compass that afternoon. When I had dropped the boltcroppers on the glass I had sealed the crack with flexible sealer. Somehow I had rubbed some of it off and a small leak must have developed, for the bubble in the glass had got very large. The liquid is present in the compass bowl to slow down the oscillations of the needle due to the boat's motion. An undamped needle would be useless on a boat as it would spin round like a mad thing, never settling long enough for one to find out where it is pointing. I don't know how the early mariners managed with their pieces of lodestone on a string.

The liquid remaining in my compass was still covering the needle-mounted card to serve its damping function, but the bubble was so large that because of peculiar refraction through the three media of liquid, air and glass it was difficult to read the numbers on the card.

I took the compass off its bracket and looked for the filling hole. This was stopped up with a large screw under which were written the words FILL ONLY WITH ALCOHOL. Now that presented a problem for I hadn't brought any clear alcohol along, not even a bottle of gin. I did have whisky and brandy. I just hoped that one of these, diluted by the liquid still in the compass, would be transparent enough to let me read the card. I decided to try. If it did not work I still had the tell-tale compass which I could mount in the cockpit.

I got out the brandy bottle, gripped the compass between my knees, unscrewed the filler screw and poured. An airlock promptly formed and brandy streamed all over my trousers. I tried again more gently and managed to fill it up, though more brandy went over my trousers than in the compass. Still, I had another five bottles of the stuff. I finished off by injecting the last few drops with a hypodermic syringe, and when I righted the compass I found that the bubble was quite tiny, a mere shadow of its former self. The card was quite legible through the peat-coloured liquid. So I fixed the compass back in its bracket and decided to use the remainder of the brandy for its proper purpose.

As I sat there drinking my brandy and lemonade cocktail I started thinking about Donald Crowhurst, who died at sea in mysterious circumstances, having pretended that he was sailing round the world when he really hadn't left the Atlantic. I hadn't read the book about him; the more people said to me 'You must read about Donald Crowhurst' the less I wanted to read it, feeling that it might be bad luck. All I knew was that he had left Teignmouth, on the south coast of England, in a trimaran to compete in the Round the World solo race. He had quickly discovered that some essential equipment had been left behind and that his boat was not sufficiently seaworthy to face the Roaring Forties, but instead of turning back he had carried on, sending out misleading messages which implied that he was doing well in the race, when he never actually left the Atlantic. His trimaran was eventually found abandoned and it was assumed that he had committed suicide.

'I haven't read the book but feel he must have been very upset before he left, since being alone tends to emphasize emotions already felt. I can understand the tendency to want to cheat — I feel it myself — but think he must have had terrific financial and emotional liabilities to be overcome by the temptation. If I had been him I would hope to have kept my nerve and staged a dramatic shipwreck, so as to keep the goodies, the glory and my life. Or would I? Perhaps I too would do the decent thing and say goodbye to life honourably. But I think I am enough of a realist and a sufficiently good self-deceiver to get away with cheating.'

I have now read the book about the voyage. They say he went mad, but by who's definition? Surely madness can only be defined as an inability to deal with one's surroundings, and Crowhurst was clearly capable of doing that. Certainly he was not 'normal'; his attitude to life changed drastically and it is probable that he did commit suicide. But one could argue that this is evidence of sanity, of an awareness that this was the best solution of his problems in the long run. It is not long since suicide was expected of a man who had got into personal or financial difficulties, and I think that Donald Crowhurst was brave enough to do it.

But he should never have ventured on this voyage without more time to get ready. His boat was ill-prepared and his reasons for going were wrong. He showed that he was not able to plan and organize effectively, and planning and organization are the basis of success in anything.

But they said that I should not have gone. If I had drowned they would have said I was foolhardy; if Crowhurst had succeeded they would have said he was a hero. Nothing succeeds like success: nothing fails like failure.

With such dismal thoughts I went to bed. At 04.30 hours I passed the thousand-mile mark on the log. By the following morning I could steer the course I wanted to take me between Terceira and Sao Miguel as the wind had veered during the night. By noon it was near enough a calm and I decided to go up the mast to get the radar reflector down so that I could do something about its sharp edges. I rigged the bosun's chair and was just hauling myself up when along came a breeze and off we went. Without taking the mainsail down I could not get a grip on the mast with my knees and so was banged around. So down I came, without the reflector. 'I have just discovered how to end a calm. Climb the mast.'

I noticed that my good alarm clock had stopped. I opened it up to have a look inside. (I can't resist opening things to see how they work.) Alas! In reassembling it I made an error and ensured that, if it hadn't been irrevocably broken before, it was now. Still, the cheap alarm and chronometer were working. Two down and two to go!

During the afternoon, becalmed again, I pottered round the deck with nothing on, soaking up the first bit of sunshine for days. I did a bit of washing and hung the clothes on one of the lifelines where it looked very gay. Then I relaxed over tea with bread and honey followed by some of my mother's parkin. Later on I ate a whole packet of cheese-spread triangles and a couple of tomatoes and only after finishing that lot did I remember that I was supposed to be having a celebration dinner that night to mark the thousand miles from home.

I remembered our celebration last year for a thousand miles out from the Azores. We had curried steak and rice, accompanied by Portuguese champagne. That was the last good meal we had as by then we were on strict rations. It was the last meat that Peter and I had, for the third member of the crew, Mike Robertson, is allergic to fish and eggs, so he got all the steak and spam while we had the eggs – very dubious – and tinned tunny fish. This time I had planned the meal before I left. I was to have prawn cocktail, asparagus, ham, new potatoes and li-chees.

After all my nibbling I couldn't face the thought of a big meal so I postponed it to the next evening.

When I woke the following morning and looked out of the cabin I could see a line of black clouds approaching. I decided that it might be a good idea to replace the genoa with the next size down, the No 1 jib. Thank goodness I did, for twenty minutes later we were hit by quite the most impressive squall I had ever experienced. The rain came down solidly, flattening the sea and soaking my trousers in a split second. I had to leap to the helm, for *Aziz* was pressed over. I bore away from the wind and ended up sailing north-east at a great rate. Not the direction I wanted for that was the way back to Britain. I gybed round and shot off south by east instead, the sky full of rain and the sea whipped up into little white horses.

As I sat there heaving on the tiller, for the sails were not trimmed properly, I felt the strain die away. The air became air again, light penetrated the sky and the white horses lay down. Soon all was peaceful and I brought *Aziz* back on to the wind and we sailed on towards the Azores.

By late afternoon it was very calm and I motored for an hour to loosen up the engine and charge the battery. I intensely dislike motoring; the noise shatters the peace of a calm sea, the boat vibrates and I have to concentrate very hard on the steering compass. A moment's inattention is enough to allow *Aziz* to whip round in a semicircle. She has practically no directional stability because she has a short keel and a separate rudder. This means that she is manoeuvrable and easily handled by the self-steering gear and by me. But it also means that she is a pig under power, and God help me if the self-steering breaks. I would have a job rigging a jury system and would probably end up steering eighteen hours a day. A nasty thought.

Trying to get a cigarette and matches out of the cabin is quite a laugh. I centre the tiller so she is steering straight, climb into the cabin, stretch out to straighten her up again, duck down to open the match locker, stretch out again to straighten her, grab the fags and leap back into the cockpit. Daft! Why didn't I throttle back so that *Aziz* was almost still? Because I was rather enjoying myself – a sort of 'beat the machine' game.

A nice breeze picked up early in the night and we went belting along slightly off the wind with the genoa doing a grand job. The breeze dropped a little in the morning but we still moved along fairly well under a grey, overcast sky.

At noon I took a sight. I can't believe it. My noon sight – taken with both sextants – puts me at 40° 46′ N which is well north of what I thought. I fear my navigation may be completely adrift – I can't pick up the Azores beacons. I might be anywhere. It is most worrying. I keep taking sights but no longer believe them. Oh, woe! I just can't be up there.'

At 15.00 hours I happened to look out of the cabin and what did I see?

A ship; a ship at last. Thank goodness. I was beginning to believe that they didn't exist. This one is about two miles away, already abeam, a grey silhouette moving steadily east against a grey haze. Quick as a flash I get out the signal lamp and gaily send off 'AA AA AA' – the call-up signal. No reply. He *must* see me. I flash again 'K K K' – 'I wish to communicate with you'. Still no reply, and now he is going away from me. Again I try, but it is no good. My heart sinks and a tear of frustration and despair comes into my eyes. 'It's not fair. Why isn't he looking?' But of course it is fair: I had spotted him too late.

Will it be another thirteen days before I see a second ship?

8   Temptation One

I was now getting close to the Azores, I thought, and at last I managed to get radio Direction Finding bearings on the beacons on Sao Miguel and Santa Maria.

The Azores are a group of nine volcanic islands rising steeply from the sea. There are three groups. The southern pair of Santa Maria and Sao Miguel are the most important from an international point of view, for Santa Maria has the international airport and Sao Miguel has the capital city Ponta Delgada. About a hundred miles west-north-west of Sao Miguel is the middle group, consisting of Terceira, Graciosa, Pico, Sao Jorge and Faial, and about a hundred miles north-west of these are the northern pair, Florez and Corvo.

The islands were uninhabited until the Portuguese colonized them in the fifteenth century. Then they became a rendezvous for the Spanish and Portuguese fleets on their way back from the New World. Consequently they were the scene of a number of battles between the English, greedy for plunder, and the Peninsular powers.

It was off Florez that the famous battle between Sir Richard Grenville in the little *Revenge* and fifty-three Spanish ships of war took place. The *Revenge* fought bravely, becalmed in the lee of a great galleon, but surrendered after fighting for fifteeen hours. The English considered it a great battle and a moral victory. English children are still taught about it in school.

The islands are now friendly to the British and we had a great welcome when we visited them last year. We arrived in Ponta Delgada ten days out from Spain and spent a week there, the crew sightseeing and the captain selling seed potatoes. Sao Miguel is the largest of the islands and, like the others, is covered with little green and yellow walled fields climbing the sides of volcanic hills. The roads are lined with blue hydrangeas and one sees as many horses and mules on them as cars.

After a week we sailed to Faial, the most perfect sail I have had. The sky was blue, the sea was sapphire, the wind was just right. We sunbathed all day and lazily watched the seas go past. Navigation was easy for the positions of the islands were clearly marked by the cap of cloud over each. Nevertheless, I was relieved when Pico and Sao Jorge duly appeared from under their bonnets, for this was the first time I had been in charge of navigation.

During the night we sailed between these two islands, craning our necks to peer at the top of Pico, a perfect volcanic cone reaching 7,600 feet. We arrived at Horta, the port of Faial, the following morning. There were several yachts tied up there, most *en route* for Europe from the West Indies but some having come the same way as us. In our ten days there we swam, saw the sights, drank in the Café Sport and visited Sao Jorge. We had a terrific welcome there for it seemed as if the whole town was on the quayside. Every move we made was commented on and despite the language problem we were shown over the island.

We then went to Santa Cruz on Florez. This had the most terrifying harbour it has been my misfortune to spend a night in. To enter the harbour you head for a narrow gap in the volcanic reef and as soon as you are through turn sharply to starboard. If you don't make this turn you end up on the cliffs, as did one British yacht whose bones are still visible. The harbour is tiny and a big swell comes in. We were moored with two lines to buoys and two lines round pinnacles of rock. *Pinta* would surge towards the rocks, our hearts would stop. Then she would surge back towards the centre of the harbour. We stayed for one sweaty night. In the morning we took in the lines from the rocks, cut the lines to the buoys and motored out to head for home. Was I glad to leave!

This time I was going to keep clear of land, but wanted to

sight one of the islands to check my position. I could not decide whether to pass between the middle and southern groups or whether to go south of the lot. If you study the winds and currents it seems that the situation is slightly more favourable if one goes south. But it is farther and on balance I thought it would be better to pass between. However, the wind was south-westerly and unless it changed I would have to tack to get north of Sao Miguel, which would hardly be worthwhile. I decided to keep as far west as possible and see how it panned out.

As usual I spent the day nibbling and listening to the radio. The news was full of the Common Market negotiations, with a statement to be made in the House of Commons about them. I became terribly well informed about such issues as I was picking up programmes from all over the world – Britain, America, Canada, South Africa, Australia and Russia. There was also a splendid religious station broadcasting from, I think, Ecuador, which did fascinating interpretations of the Scriptures.

From my position well away from it all I felt more objective about world events. I eventually decided that it would probably be a good thing if Britain joined the Common Market so that she would have a say in political and economic decisions which will affect her anyway. I also wished that they would think of another topic for discussion.

The following morning, Day 14, a radio DF fix put me about a hundred miles from Sao Miguel. I needed to steer a course of 252° True to pass north of the island but unfortunately the best I could make was 230° True, which was a nuisance. I decided to carry on and if necessary pass south of the island rather than put in a tack to the north-west. During the day the wind piped up a fraction and I was making good speed with the No 1 jib and a single reef in the main. We were pounding a bit as the bows dropped off the tops of the waves. Twice I got dressed and went out to change to a smaller jib but each time I decided that the pounding was unavoidable because there was a little short sea.

By 17.00 hours we were forty miles from Sao Miguel and the wind had backed ten degrees or so which meant I would certainly have to go south of the island. I slept for a couple of hours in the afternoon in preparation for a night of watching for a light on the land. At dusk I took an anti-sleep pill, lit the Tilley lamp and settled down to read *Lord of the Rings*. The sunset was splendid with orange and russet overhanging the horizon and a pencil-thin silver crescent drawn on a deep blue sky.

At 01.45 hours I sighted a light, bearing 241° True. This was the right bearing for the light on the north-east corner of Sao Miguel. I had made a correct landfall. The date was 26 June and I had been at sea for thirteen and a half days, so I had made quite a reasonable passage.

The night was pitch black, the sky studded with brilliants. A perfect night for picking up lights. I saw the lights of a ship going east and wondered where he was going. I sailed steadily on and passed about ten miles from the light, close enough to see the lines of street lamps in the town below the light and to watch a car's lights climb up and away.

At dawn we were still close, but cloud had formed and instead of a yellow and green jewel rising from the sea there was a blue-grey shadow squatting under a grey cloud. Nevertheless out came the camera to record the scene and prove that I really had been there. I was delighted to have made a landfall and gained conclusive evidence that I was going somewhere, and the right somewhere at that.

Once clear of the land I wanted to head west for America. I couldn't because the wind was coming from the west, so I continued on the same course, down towards Santa Maria. This soon appeared as another grey shadow. I was pleased to have sighted Santa Maria, for now I had seen all the islands in the Archipelago dos Acores.

'I am surprised how little tempted I am to close land and have a look at it. I would have liked to see the green and yellow strip fields and the little volcanic peaks, but all I can see is a blue-grey outline of both islands . . . This is the end of Stage 1 and the beginning of Stage 2, which involves going due west

for about 40° of longitude . . . I wish I had been able to pass
a message as I'm afraid my parents will be worrying.'

I had actually gone to the lengths of writing a message
addressed to the harbour master and putting it in a Tupperware
box with a couple of packets of cigarettes. I hoped that I would
be able to give it to a passing fishing boat so naturally I didn't
see any sort of vessel at all. I was regularly flown over by the
ferry plane from Santa Maria to Sao Miguel and each time
waved furiously. I imagined the passengers seeing my little boat
beneath them and wondering where I was going. They wouldn't
guess that I was heading for America.

I tacked between the islands and headed back towards Sao
Miguel. The wind was very light by now so I lowered the
mainsail to do a few repairs. The second batten pocket had
worn through at the inner end. I mended it by putting a layer
of adhesive sail tape over it, then stitching a square of Terylene
cloth over that and finally putting another layer of tape round
the edges of the patch. This took quite a long time as the cloth
was stiff and I was in an awkward position on the cabin roof.

I replaced all the battens except the first as they were broken.
I had to cut a new second batten from a length of Tufnol-type
strip. This had a bend in it from being stowed bent in the
forward cabin which gave the sail an odd shape. I hoped it
would straighten out, and it did within a few hours.

At 18.30 hours I was quite close again to Sao Miguel and
through the binoculars I could clearly see Ponta Delgada. Now
I was tempted to go close to see if I could pass a message, but
did not dare for I could just imagine what might happen. 'I'll
just go a little closer to have a look' and then 'I'll just sail
around the harbour' and then, before I knew what had happened, I would be sitting in a café drinking a glass of wine. No!
I resolutely put *Aziz* on to the other tack and headed away
from land.

I slept like a log that night and woke at 06.00 hours feeling
very well. It was a sparkling day with a milky-blue sea and a
few clouds over where the islands must be. The wind had
veered and I was actually able to sail due west which made me
very happy.

In the morning I washed my hair, taking a couple of photographs of the process. I filled the bucket with sea water, put it on the cockpit floor, and stood in the cabin leaning out into the cockpit. When I had finished I rinsed about a pint of fresh water through my hair to get rid of the salt. The result was marvellous. I felt a new woman. I then did a bit of sunbathing, trying to get an all-over tan, but I soon got a bit burned so gave up the life of the idle rich and went back to work.

I hauled myself up the mast to get the radar reflector down so that I could give it an anti-chafe treatment. It was rather nice up there and I got a new view of *Aziz*. I could see her below me idly nosing through the wavelets. She looked like a broad white dart moving graciously beneath my feet, quite at ease with her world.

I took the radar reflector into the cabin where I bound the edges with two layers of insulating tape, topped with a layer of thin green plastic tape to stop the black stickiness of the insulating tape from dirtying the sails. I put extra layers over the corners and was quite pleased with the result. It used rather a lot of tape but was worth it if it stayed on.

Getting the thing re-attached to the shrouds was quite a problem. I needed three hands for getting the last shackle pin in; one to hold the reflector, one to hold the shroud and the third to hold the pin. I had a hell of a struggle and once dropped the pin to the deck. I had to go down to pick it up and found I was getting quite tired when I hauled myself up again. Damn thing. I couldn't get it in. I was just about to give up and fetch some wire to use instead when Hey Presto! – there it was, all together and shipshape. I felt much better for having done that job for it had been on my conscience for a long time.

I saw some dolphins in the distance leaping above the horizon and splashing down in a fountain of white spray. I whistled to them to come closer but they had business elsewhere. I love dolphins because they are so joyful, leaping about with gay abandon.

I still had caught no fish despite trailing a line most of the time. I had lost several lures – a spinner, a spoon and a plastic worm — so I knew that there were big fish about. Still, what would I do with a two-hundred-pound tuna?

The next morning I found myself absolutely stationary under a brilliant sky. I soon discovered that I had company, a large shoal of small fish which gathered round the boat. The sea was clear and I could see, suspended beneath me, small organisms and jelly fish. The log line hung like a plumb line into the deeps.

The sun was very hot and I stripped off to potter about the deck, photographing the fish and trying to catch one. They were very inquisitive and would rush up to inspect every titbit I offered them. Clearly they were fish of discrimination, for everything I offered was turned down: cheese, rice, tomato, steak and biscuit. The shoal grew and grew in size until it was like sailing in a hatchery. Most of the fish flicked lazily to and fro but one appeared to have something wrong for it swam furiously on the surface leaving a trail of ripples. I wondered at first if it was some sort of courtship dance, but eventually concluded that it had sunstroke.

I enjoyed that day of idling around. I didn't mind being becalmed for I had expected it to happen. I had had plenty of experience of drifting around with no power. On the return trip from the Azores we only recorded one-fifth of a mile on the log one day. Coming back from Ireland a fortnight before leaving on this trip I had been becalmed and spent a night and a day drifting round the islands off the Pembrokeshire coast. That was nerve-racking for the tides run strongly there and at one time I thought I was going to end up on the rocks. However I was finally towed in to a safe mooring.

The next day was pretty calm and I spent this one painting the iron bracket supporting the self-steering vane. I had put several coats of metallic primer on at Dale but had not had time for a top coat. Now I painted it white which smartened up the ugly structure a bit. It was quite a job for I had to contort myself to reach all the parts without falling over. I succeeded in getting white streaks in my hair but managed to avoid spilling the paint over the deck.

There was a light following wind so I raised twin foresails

Aziz about to be launched for the trip to Ireland

The last morning – preparing to leave

Leaving the beach for the last time

With stores a few days before leaving

Coiling rope in the cockpit

Taking a sextant sight

Under way – 4,000 miles to go

Looking out from the cabin

Making *Aziz* ship-shape at Newport, Rhode Island

A shambles below deck

A sight to remember

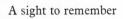

and dropped the main. The foresails were held outstretched by poles and seemed to be quite effective. *Aziz* was yawing about rather a lot because the wind was too light to swing the self-steering vane until we were a long way off course. One really wants to increase the vane area in these conditions and I think an extension would be worthwhile if one expected a lot of downwind sailing. It would not be difficult to fix up. Now why didn't I do so? My brain must have been addled by the sun.

I heard on the radio that day that Chay Blyth had completed his technical circumnavigation, crossing his outward track somewhere south-west of the Cape Verde Islands. He had sailed the 'wrong' way round against the Roaring Forties. Good for him; that must have been quite a trip.

The following morning there was sadder news. The three Russian cosmonauts who had been longer in space than any others had died during re-entry. What a tragedy.

I counted my unread books and found that I still had over a dozen left. I seemed to be getting through about one a day as there was a lot of time to fill in, a problem that I had not anticipated. 'In fact, although I am not lonely I do get rather bored and could do with someone to talk to. Thank goodness for the radio. I think I would go potty without it, but think I am quite sane now, though becoming more impulsive over little things than before while more thoughtful about bigger things. Perhaps I am just getting a better sense of proportion.'

During the night the wind rose to a sturdy Force 4–5 from the south-west and quite a large swell appeared. By noon the next day I was down to the No 2 jib and three reefs in the main. It was a most frustrating day as I couldn't sail close to the wind without great hammerings and slammings and so spent the day going north and south and not getting very far west. I made a tactical error here for I should have stuck to the southern tack and made some southing instead of trying to stay in the same latitude. I was a little too far north, too near the main flow of the Gulf Stream and would have done better to keep away from it.

The bows were dipping under the water at times and water flooded over the foredeck up the cabin roof, and quite large lumps ended up in the cabin. The forehatch was leaking and I could see dollops of water spurting through onto the stores. I made a mental note to put some sealer round the edge of the hatch when the foredeck was dry.

During the night I had a vivid dream about going ashore on Florez to send a message home. It did not look like Florez but was more like one of the Shetland Isles with great cliffs rising out of a ruff of spray. I went into the post office but they wouldn't accept my English money. Then I found myself in a tiny shop trying to buy a packet of Gauloises cigarettes. They had shelves and shelves of them in various coloured packets, but none in the traditional blue. I was very worried about *Aziz* being out on the wild sea alone. Most confusing. As usual in my dreams I was aware of my real situation and had no escape from it.

Wind and sea moderated the next day and by evening I had full main and No 2 jib up. I didn't do much apart from reading, but spent the afternoon listening to the final of the Women's Singles at the Wimbledon Tennis Championships. It was a very exciting match in which the young Australian, Evonne Goolagong, just beat Margaret Smith. The radio was working well in spite of having hit the floor with a hideous crash the previous day.

About eleven-thirty that night the log reached 2,000 miles. It had taken twenty and a half days. The first thousand had taken ten days so my speed through the water was about the same. The speed over the ground was unfortunately less as I had done quite a lot of tacking. I worked out that I had done 1,500 miles along my planned route and had another 2,000 to go. At this rate of progress it would take me another four weeks which was longer than I had hoped.

The next day was Saturday 3 July. I had been at sea for three weeks. I hadn't spoken to anyone. I was getting worried that I never would speak to anyone and would eventually turn up in America completely out of the blue.

About half past one I popped my head out of the cabin and there was a ship. She was abeam of me and travelling in the same direction. Out comes the lamp. I signal 'AA AA AA', the call-up signal. No reply. I try again. No answer. I start sending 'K K K', thinking that perhaps they have mislaid their signal lamp. Now she is across my bows, about a mile away. 'Please answer.' I keep sending but there is no response and gradually my excitement dies. I shake my fist at her and retire below in a huff to listen to tennis on the radio. Doesn't anyone keep a lookout?

I sit on the settee berth, light a cigarette and plug in the earphones. The match is fascinating and I am totally absorbed in it. Then 'Hoot! Hoot!' A ship's foghorn.

I leap into the cockpit and there is my ship, about a hundred yards away on the port quarter, moving at the same speed as I am. I wave, then dive below for the loudhailer. I can see a number of people waving and I wave back, grinning all over my face like a Cheshire cat.

I think the captain wants me to slow down but I don't do so as I think it is much safer if we both have manoeuvring speed. He closes in. I nearly run under his bows but sheer off in time. Now we are about fifty feet apart.

I ask him to report me to London. He says he will in a good British accent, so I believe him. Then I ask for my position and he tells me that we are at 37° 48′ N, 33° 37′ W. I tell him that I am on my way to America and that I am single-handed. He doesn't seem surprised, but asks if I need anything. I say, 'No thank you. Thank you very much for stopping', and wave goodbye.

As he draws ahead of me I can see that he is the *Port Melbourne* from London, so I feel confident that the message will get through.

It would certainly simplify things if the new International Code of Signals had an equivalent to the old MIK signal which meant 'Please report me to Lloyd's of London'. There would then be no need to stop a ship just to report one's existence. I am very grateful to the captain of the *Port Melbourne*, for it would have cost him time and money slowing down his engines and then getting up speed again.

I felt delighted that my parents and friends would know

that I am still alive. It cheered me up a lot to talk to someone; three weeks is a long time to be totally alone.

As soon as the ship left me it was time to take a noon sight. It gave a latitude of 37° 51′ N, only three miles different from the latitude given me. Not bad at all. It might be him that is out. My latitude, brought forward from the morning sight, is only ten miles out. Not bad either. It is nice to know that my navigation is only miles out and not degrees.

9 *Talking to Myself*

Although we were going along at a great lick under genoa and main I soon changed down to the No 1 jib, wondering what was coming, for there was a windy sky strewn with cloud from the south-west horizon. However, the wind died away and by dusk I was heading south with a very light wind although the sky portended more enthusiastic conditions.

I stayed with the No 1 jib all through the night and eventually the wind arrived, rather more than I had bargained for, with two vicious squalls with heavy rain during the early hours. Then the wind died away completely. Dawn was ominous, a great red ball rising under high dark clouds with orange reflections on them. The sea was very slight and as a breeze picked up from the south-south-west we moved very easily. 'If one could sail on a sea of mercury which did not ripple one could go like the clappers even in a storm, as it is sea and not wind which stops a boat . . . I think I will take up high-performance dinghy sailing on reservoirs!'

By midday the wind was quite strong, Force 5 or 6, and the sea had risen. There were plenty of white horses and occasionally a wave would break over the side and into the cockpit. I had reduced sail to No 2 jib and three reefs in the main and we were still going along pretty fast. Before reefing I reckoned I was doing seven knots at times, which was very exciting. *Aziz* pitched and rolled and I had a job keeping steady enough to get a decent sight at noon.

During the afternoon the wind veered through forty degrees and I was heading about west-north-west, about seventy degrees off the wind at a speed of five and a half knots. When I tried to get closer to the wind there was a terrible pounding as *Aziz* tried to cope with a spiky sea caused apparently by swells from two directions. Once I was caught standing in the cabin and not holding on and suddenly found myself hurled against the side. I hit my head on one of the bolts round the windows and caught my knee a terrific crack against the table.

There was a terrific noise of *Aziz* pounding on the waves, things rattling around, the rigging creaking and the water rushing past. I could not listen to the radio unless I lay in my bunk as the radio was behind my pillow to stop it sliding to the floor. As it was Sunday I had a hymn-singing session instead, and went through a considerable repertoire. I found that it made me quite emotional and could hardly get through the sailors' hymn 'Eternal Father'. However, it was good for morale except that I found that I was singing out of tune.

It upset me to be out of tune as I have always had good pitch. I used to do a lot of choral singing at school and university, which I enjoyed, and was worried that my vocal chords might have atrophied. I wondered if I was, in fact, talking to myself. I hadn't been aware of doing so but I was certainly thinking very loudly. I decided that I wasn't actually speaking when I found that I could think just as loudly while eating at the same time. About the only things I did say aloud were short, sharp expletives when something went awry. My voice sounded quite strange.

The singing that day set me off thinking about my university days. I started in Bristol in 1961 studying physics, the subject I had always liked best at school. Alas, when I reached university level I was completely out of my depth because it was so mathematical. I had been reasonably good at maths at school but was totally bewildered by the lectures I was now attending. Admittedly this was not wholly due to an innate lack of understanding but also to the distracting influence of first love. Anyway, I failed all my exams at the end of the first year.

The authorities were kind and allowed me to stay, but I had to find a new subsidiary subject to replace applied maths. I selected psychology. I knew nothing about it but thought it might be interesting to find out. I took to it immediately. I was particularly interested in how people perceive the physical world. I also enjoyed ethology, the study of the behaviour of animals in their natural environment, but I never had much sympathy with the rats-in-cages type of animal psychology, and none at all with the physiological psychologists who maim animals to satisfy their curiosity.

Because of my mechanical bent I went into applied experimental psychology when I graduated. I enjoyed the work very much although it involved little of the layman's 'psychology': personality studies, psychoanalysis, group psychology and so on. Originally I took a very mechanical approach to the human being, concerned only with what goes in, and what comes out in response, not with what goes on inside. Now I realize that personal and social factors are supremely important in determining how an individual will react. It is no wonder that psychology is still a disorganized body of knowledge. Predicting a single person's behaviour is like a physicist trying to predict what a single molecule is going to do, but is vastly more complex because all an individual's past experience will affect his reaction.

I have spent all my working life doing research of one kind or another. I now realized that the things I enjoyed most have been the craftsman side of the job, not the academic side. I like the art of designing experiments so that the results will be informative. I like designing and building apparatus. I like doing statistical analysis, which is a craft and not a science.

Having detached myself from the academic world, with its posing and pretensions, I could see that I do not really have a scientific mind. While I am fascinated by ideas I am more interested in personal truth than 'objective' truth. I adore intelligent discussion for its own sake, for the pleasure I get from striking sparks between my mind and others. I do not have the singlemindedness to concentrate on a small aspect of knowledge, as a scientist must.

Aziz bucketed through the night while I slept. By morning the wind had increased to a hearty Force 6, so I changed from the No 2 jib to the No 3. This change did not seem to make much difference to our headlong flight so I took off the No 3 and we ambled along at about two knots. The No 2 was old and baggy and the No 3 was new and shapely so I suppose they were giving about the same amount of lift despite the difference in area. There would have been more drag from the No 2 and so from now on I rarely used it for windward work.

It was much more comfortable with no headsail and I was particularly pleased because my bunk no longer got dollops of spray on it. I modified my jib-changing technique for heavy weather so that I didn't have to go on the foredeck while *Aziz* was in full flight. It was very difficult to work on because of the jerky motion and the solid water pouring over one. Now I got the jib down and lashed to the rails before taking the sail bags forward, and similarly removed the bags before hoisting the new sail. This needed more stages but was probably no more time consuming as I could work more efficiently.

Now that we were almost hove to I could hear the waves breaking. They sounded like a heavy sigh – Ssssshhh – and I noticed that the ones that hit the boat were usually not audible, only the ones that passed astern. I wondered what it would be like in really heavy seas such as those in the Southern Ocean. I could imagine them coming like an express train to crash hideously over the decks.

We had logged 128 miles in the twenty-four hours to 10.00 hours, at an average of five and one-third knots, which was not bad going, and most of it in the right direction. The noon-to-noon run by sights – that is, in a straight line – was 106 miles. I was rather pleased to have done so well despite the weather.

During the afternoon the wind veered gradually through ninety degrees and eased a little, and at 19.00 hours the barometer started to rise, so I raised the No 3 jib. An hour later I unreefed to the first batten and by midnight I had full main and No 1 jib and was going nicely in a Force 2–3 north-westerly.

At 01.00 hours I could see dark clouds ahead and shortly after there was a brief squall with a rush of wind, followed by a calm during which I dropped the mainsail because the boom was thrashing from side to side as *Aziz* rolled. After a while the wind started to rise again, and with it the sea, and by the next afternoon we were back to a Force 5–6 from the north-east, after which it dropped a little and carried on veering.

By midnight we were almost on a dead run with a Force 3 wind so I took down the main and hoisted the No 1 jib as a twin for the No 2. It turned out to be quite a battle for as I hauled up the sail with the wind still coming from astern it flew forward pulling out the whole length of the sheet. Then it blew across to the wrong side dragging the sheet under the bows. *Aziz* promptly sailed over it and the sheet became wrapped round the rudder. Nasty.

I got out a spinnaker sheet, clipped it on to the errant jib and the same thing nearly happened again. I managed to tame the beast and get the sail drawing. Then I unclipped the original sheet, untied the knot in the cockpit end and hauled it in. Luckily it did not jam between the rudder and the hull for that would really have created problems. I don't know how I would have got it free. I might have had to go over the side and try to pull it loose.

Having sorted that lot out I tried to put a pole on the No 1 to keep it spread out. The wind was too strong for me and I couldn't get the inner end hooked on to the mast. This requires brute strength as I hadn't fitted any uphauls, downhauls or outhauls to my poles.

Next morning, I found two flying fish on deck, each about one inch long. 'It is like magic, these things happening to me when I have read about them happening to the heroes.'

I also found a messy lump of oil on the foredeck, which was a nasty surprise. I hadn't seen any signs of it floating about but suppose that most bits are too small to be easily visible. The water was very clean and clear, and there were no signs of the pollution that people had predicted I would find.

I took sights in the morning and at noon and fixed my position as 37° 39′ N, 41° 13′ W. This was my twenty-sixth day out. At last I could change charts from one showing Europe and the Atlantic to one showing the Atlantic and America.

'Hooray! It is nice to have my destination on the chart instead of my starting point.'

10 Scare

I was standing in the cockpit idly viewing the panorama of blue sky and sea when out of the corner of my eye I saw a brown splodge floating past. It looked like seaweed but was gone before I could tell. Then I saw another splodge approaching, and sure enough it was weed. It was yellow ochre in colour and appeared to consist of small bladders attached to one another by raffia. I was very surprised to see it there for I thought it was the type of weed found in the Sargasso Sea, well away to the south-west. I could only assume that it had drifted up in the Gulf Stream, being unwilling to suppose that my navigation was that far out.

I expected that these few pieces were just around by chance but soon discovered that the whole ocean was scattered with such bits of weed. I got used to it being around and having to clear it off the log line, and saw it every day until I was the other side of the Gulf Stream. I wanted to catch a piece in the bucket to see whether there was any marine life attached to it for I had read stories of little crabs and miniature monsters living in floating weed. However I did not dare risk my only bucket in such a venture so never found out if such stories were true. The pieces cut from the log line were deserted as one would expect, for spinning round and round is not a natural mode of life for any creature.

That afternoon I discovered a tragedy. I was poking around the forward cabin searching for the container of Ryvita packets when I noticed that the lower stowage on the starboard side had about three inches of evil-looking browny-orange liquid in it. It turned out to be a mixture of paraffin and orange juice. I assumed that the paraffin had been lurking somewhere since the original spillage, for since then I had kept the containers in the cockpit. The orange juice came from a plastic bottle which had cracked at the edge of a dent.

The tragedy was that this unappetizing liquid had found its way into the large square tin which contained a considerable quantity of fruit cake and parkin which my mother had baked for me. Fortunately she had wrapped everything in aluminium foil so the penetration was limited, but I had to cut off the outside layer of each cake. The parkin was easy to remedy for it had changed colour where it was wet, but the fruit cake was difficult as it was rich and damp to start with.

To cap my anger at this despoiling of my goodies I managed to cover the cockpit with crumbs and mixed fruit by misjudging my throw when jettisoning the soggy bits. Yuk! I sat down and sulked.

Next morning I was sleeping peacefully when I was suddenly brought to consciousness by a thump above my head, immediately followed by a lot of fluttering. I thought that a whole flight of flying fish must have come aboard and lay there for a few moments listening to the fluttering and anticipating fresh fish. Then I dragged myself out of the bunk and climbed into the cockpit.

One solitary flying fish lay on the seat, fluttering his fins spasmodically. He had a bloody nose and I guessed that he had flown into the side of the cockpit. I tried to pick it up so that I could hit it on the head and kill it quickly but it flapped so much that I couldn't get hold of it. After a few rather tentative tries I gave up and left it to suffocate. I went back to bed thinking that when I got up it would be dead and I could eat it for breakfast.

I felt rather cowardly leaving it there to die slowly, for it brought to mind one of the times when I really despised myself. I was driving near Salisbury Plain when a game bird of some sort leaped out of the hedge into my windscreen. A mess of red and yellow fluid blotted out my vision, but I felt the lump hit the roof before bouncing off. It went in a high arc and I watched through the rear-view mirror as it dropped to the road behind me, a whirling mess of feathers.

I wanted to go back to see whether it was still alive, but couldn't force myself to do so in case it was, and drove on feeling a real worm. I should have gone back, and hope that if it happens again I would do so. I am sure familiarity with such situations enables one to control one's responses and act in a more reasonable way. I don't like killing or hurting any living thing though I am sure I could learn to do so for food or pity. I would hate to learn to kill for sport.

My flying fish was delicious fried in butter. I could have done with about three more. This one was the first I had seen of an edible size. It was about seven inches long, silver below and navy blue above, with a blunt nose and, of course, the wings. These are really overdeveloped pectoral fins and act as gliding planes rather than true wings. When spread out the fish has a silhouette similar to a World War II Spitfire, the wings being quite broad and curved on the trailing edges. I never saw any flying exhibitions, but occasionally saw small fish skitter upwind when frightened by *Aziz* pounding up on them.

Luck was with me that morning. When I went out to fetch in my breakfast I noticed that the topping lift, a line from the end of the boom to the masthead and down to the base of the mast, had come unshackled from the boom. The two ends of the lift were wrapped round the port shrouds, fortunately within my reach for had they not been I would have had to do some acrobatics to get them down. The shackle which had come undone was stainless steel and I replaced it with a large bronze one. I hadn't wired the pin of the stainless one, which I should have done. Unlike bronze and galvanized shackles, stainless ones do not corrode and jam solid.

I looked over the side and found that some large fish were swimming under the boat. At first I thought they were dolphin. They weren't. There were five of them, each about four feet long and with the characteristic side fins of the shark family. It was odd that I noticed them just after I had cleaned out the flying fish over the side. I made sure that I didn't put my hands over the side lest they fancy a taste of my blood.

They stayed with me at least till lunchtime, when a breeze ruffled the water and I could no longer see them. They didn't do very well out of me for the only scraps I offered them were the bones of my fish.

I spent a domestic afternoon, washing everything I could lay hands on: dishes, clothes, my hair, myself. It was a perfect drying day, sunny and breezy, and despite being washed in salt water the clothes dried pretty well. My hair felt a lot better, a change from the nasty sticky rats' tails it usually was. It was then about shoulder length and I was tempted at times to cut it short so that it wouldn't get tangled and would keep out of my eyes. But vanity always won. I had been growing it for about two years and it was just reaching a reasonable length, being very slow growing. I knew that if I cut it off in a fit of pique I would regret it later, so I put up with the nasty sticky string that it turned into whenever the weather was bad.

During the afternoon I saw a tanker quite close, about a mile away. I signalled to him but got no reply as he steamed on towards Europe. I was not so distressed this time because of having passed a message a few days earlier. It is quite probable that he saw me but did not reply because of the trouble it would take. I could not blame him for this, for I was not sending distress signals which he would have been obliged to respond to. Still, it would have been nice of him to stop.

I worked out an arrival date based on my average progress so far. It came to sixteen days hence, which was 24 July. That would be forty-two days altogether, the time I had guestimated it would take. So I was up to schedule so far.

I was rather sorry to think that the voyage was more than half over. I had really settled down to the life, and could hardly imagine anything different. I could understand now how the real long-distance boys had endured being alone for so long. I was able to fill my days quite happily and no longer thought much about others. I felt quite detached from the world of people. Although the radio kept me well informed I did not feel concerned about current affairs.

I found that I was detached from time. Dates were merely names to identify days with and not markers of the passage of time. When I heard on the radio that some event was due to take place in August I would think: 'But why are they telling us that, it is a long time away.'

Associated with this feeling of being stationary in time was a feeling of being stationary in space. When I looked at the eastern horizon I did not really believe that there was all that sea there and that I had crossed it. I felt that I was in the same place with the sea moving past me; there was no sense of progressing.

The evening brought a sweet-and-sour experience. Shortly before dusk I signalled a ship which was heading west. She flashed back immediately, which rather impressed me. Then she altered course towards me slowing down as she approached. She was still moving quite fast as she overtook me to leeward and crossed my bows; I was afraid that she would carry on without letting me pass a message. However she stopped dead about half a mile ahead and lay there, wallowing.

It took me quite a time to sail up to her, for the wind was light, and like a fool I aimed to go up the windward side. At the last moment I realized that this was not a very good idea as I might easily run out of manoeuvring space. I sailed round her stern, a peculiar affair with great gates, and saw her name; *Lash Turkiye* of New York. I sailed up her starboard side and hailed them through the loudhailer. I got a reply but could not see where it came from. However, I requested that he report me to Lloyd's of London and he said he would. I explained that I was single-handed to Newport, Rhode Island, and he asked me if I wanted anything. I said no thank you and thanks for stopping, and as I had by now almost overtaken him I waved goodbye and put back on my course.

It was now getting dark and we both had our navigation lights on. I kept a close watch on the ship and noticed that she remained stationary for a while and then started moving off on her original course. Now it was quite dark and I could only see her lights. Suddenly I noticed that the pattern of lights was changing. Now I could see both red and green lights and that meant she was heading straight for me. I waited for her to swing round but she didn't.

'Hellfire, she is coming straight for me.' I got out the torch and shone it from the cockpit to supplement my white stern light, thinking that perhaps she hadn't realized where I was. Still she kept on coming. I started to sweat. Her lights got closer. I flashed her with the signal lamp and immediately she replied. Alas, I cannot read Morse and didn't know what she meant. At least she knew that I was there. But still she came on and now her lights were looming over me. I hastily unhitched the self-steering and swung *Aziz* around until I was heading back for England!

She got the message then and turned back on to her course and soon her lights vanished over the horizon. I expect she wondered what I was playing at. I certainly couldn't work out what she was up to. I was very grateful to her for stopping, but did 'go off' big ships for a while.

11 *A Visitor*

The next morning I got out the Admiralty Pilot for the East Coast of America. If anyone is looking for horror stories let him invest in an Admiralty Pilot. For sheer matter-of-fact spine-chilling comment there is nothing to beat them. One finds such phrases as 'small ships have been known to founder under such conditions'. This sounds bad enough for a yachtsman and quite horrifying when one realizes that their idea of a small ship is something about 200 feet long. One of my favourites concerns a narrow passage between two islands. It warns the helmsman to keep a steady course for if he does not he will be 'swept on to the rocks to almost certain destruction'.

The Pilot for America made pretty nasty reading, particularly when describing the weather. Apparently there is a corridor just off the coast up which depressions rush one after the other, bringing rapid changes in conditions. There is a small chance of hurricanes during July and a much greater chance during August. There is also a very high probability of encountering fog, an unattractive prospect.

For comparison I read the West Coast of England Pilot. That sounded pretty horrifying too so I was a little consoled, for I know that the weather there is frequently very pleasant.

I acquired an escort of three pilot fish. At least, I assumed they were pilot fish as they had very marked stripes. These went round the body instead of along it and they looked as though they were wearing football jerseys. They were very curious and would rush out from beneath *Aziz* to examine every bit of rubbish that I threw over. I didn't try to catch them as I had become rather disillusioned about my skill as a fisherman. Besides, it would have been rather inhospitable. I am not sure that they were pilot fish; somehow they looked too vulgar to fit my image.

The next day, 10 July, Day 29, was still quiet with little wind. I took advantage of the dry decks to fibreglass the forehatch lid, which was crumbling at the edges. It was poorly designed, as the circular lid was held down only by a lashing to an eye in the centre of the lid. It was consequently deformed allowing water to penetrate under the edges. I made a rather crude repair by putting a fibreglass matting over the faulty patches and soaking it with resin. The resin set so quickly after the hardener was added that I hardly had time to transfer it from the pot to the repair before it went tacky. I suppose the temperature was too high. However the result, if not beautiful, looked strong. I also bolted an eye to the inside of the cabin roof so that I could hang the Tilley lamp up.

I was having a well-deserved rest, reading a fascinating book about children growing up, and placidly crunching a clear mint sweet, when I realized that my mouth felt strange. I poked about with my tongue and discovered that a large chunk had disappeared from my left upper back tooth. Getting out my powder compact I squinted in the tiny mirror, dragging my lip back to see what the extent of the damage was. As far as I could tell the filling in the tooth was still intact and the break was not under the gum, so it was not as vast a rock fall as I had thought.

It didn't hurt which was a good thing as I had no Novocaine with me. As I had had a hole in that tooth for years, before having it filled specially for this voyage, and had never had any pain from it, I was hopeful that I wouldn't suffer now. It would be rather unheroic to give up the venture because of toothache.

I was up several times during the night for a good breeze had arrived. There were a few squalls which I nursed *Aziz* through. After one of these sorties out on deck I switched on the radio and discovered that reception was quite superb. I picked up domestic stations from Europe on the medium- and long-wave bands. I listened to 'Late Night Extra' on BBC 2 and was able to hear the 00.30 hours (BST) shipping forecast for

British waters which was interesting. They said that there was a ridge of high pressure from the Azores to the western approaches to the Channel, which agreed with what I had surmised. It was nice to hear the familiar style of the domestic BBC. I was then about 2,300 miles from the transmitter.

The following morning I saw a polythene bag floating past and thought it was a sign of the pollution we hear so much about. It wasn't. On closer inspection this bag turned out to be a Portuguese man of war, a fascinating and deadly creature. It looks rather like a jellyfish with a 'sail' running diagonally across its back and has long tendrils hanging down. These are extremely poisonous. It is not, in fact, a single animal but is a colony of several hundreds of individuals living an interdependent existence. This one was out of bounds for they usually stay within the trade-wind belts nearer the equator.

A little later I had a visitor, an elegant tern who headed straight for the boat and flew around. He seemed rather tired and tried to make a landing on the masthead. This was a real comedy act. He would fly downwind, swing round and make a run upwind, looking like an aircraft on a bombing run. As he approached *Aziz* up would go his wings, down would come his feet and – oops! the masthead would whip away from his hopeful feet and off he would go for another try. No joy!

After five or six goes he gave up and flew around looking rather forlorn. I hoped he would land on the deck but he didn't even try. Too shy, I suppose. After about twenty minutes he veered off and flew away to the south. I hope he knew that there was no land that way for thousands of miles.

That evening I had a smart cocktail hour. I dressed up in a mini dress, put on make-up, brushed my hair free of tangles and doused myself with perfume. I felt gorgeous! I had acquired a splendid all-over tan, but had difficulty in finding how dark it was as I was without the normal bikini marks. Eventually I found two white stripes under the rings I always wear, one on each hand. These were both presents and I would look at them and think about the donors. This would bring back memories of good times afloat and ashore. They seemed like scenes remembered from a film.

The next day was 12 July. I had been at sea for a calendar month. I was surprised how quickly the previous ten days had passed, and I hoped that the next ten days would go as quickly. Yet I had no feeling of covering distance. It was as if I was the centre of the world; all things were relative to me. I could see no boundary to the ocean and my chart was folded so that no land appeared on it. I was the only person in my world.

The barometer started to fall in the afternoon and the wind rose from the south-south-west to a healthy Force 4–5. We were screaming along at six and a half knots with the genoa set, but the self-steering was not happy and I changed down to the No 2 jib. There were a number of squalls which brought brief increases in wind speed. They were like angry cats spitting and hissing as they scampered across the sky.

Aziz kept falling off waves, a most unpleasant sensation. There is the suspense as you become weightless and then a hideous crash as the bows smite the water. I had to nurse her through some of the squalls and was very cross with one which sprayed salt water into my cup of lemon tea. It was quite undrinkable. Very bad manners.

The wind increased in the night and I was roused out to put three reefs in the main. I wrote in the navigation log 'previously going like a runaway racehorse' so it must have been wild. I was not prone to writing such comments in the log. Usually I stuck to factual information.

At dawn I put on the storm jib and three hours later I hove to on the port tack. The wind was now Force 6–7, still from the south-west. The seas were not particularly high, perhaps ten or twelve feet, but steep enough to be uncomfortable. Not many broke over *Aziz* though the bows dipped beneath the crests at times.

Shortly after heaving to there was torrential rain with strong gusts of wind. That was the final fling. The sky brightened, the rain stopped, and the wind veered and eased. Soon *Aziz* was moving again with a north-easterly Force 4.

I was glad the squalls had gone away for I found them rather frightening. There would be a sudden burst of wind and torrential rain which blotted out the horizon and reduced my world to a few square yards of streaming surging steely water. My inexperience frightened me for I could only guess how I should handle the boat and whether I was asking too much of her.

I had really dropped myself in at the deep end, undertaking this trip, and was quickly learning about sailing and about fear. I am not infinitely brave, as some people would have me. There was no place for bravery out there, for bravery is the wilful acceptance of a challenge. It is a reaction to pride and fear. Without fear there is no challenge: without bravery no need to accept the challenge. Yes, it was brave to set out, but now there was no choice. I could not refuse the challenge for life itself was the prize.

But would there be a limit to the amount of fear I could stand? Would fear – fear of death – finally break the unity of mind, body and reality which is sanity?

I must face reality and accept the fears and the joys and the boredoms. I must not weaken.

12   *Bad Weather Coming*

I made good progress in spite of the squalls and discovered that I had achieved an average speed of over five knots in the twenty-four hours up to 18.30 hours. This was gratifying and compensated for the discomfort involved. The temperature had dropped quite noticeably so I went back to wearing trousers, a little sadly, for I guessed that this was the end of my Garden of Eden sailing.

I had spent much of the previous weeks in a state of undress, for the skin is a comfortable and practical covering. It dries quickly when wet, it is easy to keep clean, and it is cool in the heat of the day. Often when I had to change a foresail I would undress rather than put on my oilskins to save getting anything wet. The only disadvantage of this was that I had to kneel on the foredeck, which had a rough surface. This was decidedly uncomfortable at first but after a while the skin on my knees and the top of my feet hardened up.

The main disadvantage of skin is that it is not very resistant to abrasion. However, I had become sufficiently at one with *Aziz* to avoid many severe collisions with her. I was frequently bruised for that is unavoidable. My legs had a magnificent display of purple, blue, yellow and brown splodges. My substitute for modern art.

I enjoyed the freedom of nakedness and became unaware of it as an unusual mode of dress. I was caught out on one occasion. I sighted a ship on the horizon and leaped out into the cockpit to wave. Then I hurriedly leapt back into the cabin to cover myself. Unfortunately for them they were too far away to have enjoyed the mid-ocean Follies!

I spent much of the day listening to 'Voice of America' on

the radio. I finally turned it off in disgust when they started for the third time a 'Special English' programme on the functioning of the heart. I could appreciate that the words must be simple, because the programme was aimed at people who do not know English well, but I could not understand why the concepts were so oversimplified. I am afraid the producer had not resisted the temptation to assume that lack of language ability means lack of intelligence. However, this warned me not to fall into the opposite trap, assuming that because Americans speak the same language as I do they have the same culture and standards.

I was eagerly looking forward to meeting Americans on their home ground and discovering more of what America really is. We get a very odd view through our news media. If one were to believe what one hears one would think that America is full of hippies, rioting students, rioting Negroes, rioting prisoners, snatch thieves, murderers, corrupt police, bodies lying ignored in the streets, drug takers, drug pushers, striking workers; and a huge materialist, unthinking over-friendly mass of once-divorced middle-class vegetables. And, of course, magnificent scenery.

I wouldn't be surprised if Americans have much the same view of Europe. Perhaps they are more charitable. I think that there is great envy of America in Europe, as well as a certain feeling of being more civilized – sour grapes, perhaps.

The following day was a work day. I cleared up a fair bit of the untidiness that had started to offend my eye. At last I cleared out the sawdust and wood shavings from the cooker well, remnants of Brian's strengthening of the bulkhead. I had neglected this job before as it involved taking the gas burner off its gimbals, the bearings which allow it to swing. This was not particularly difficult, requiring only a bit of levering with a screwdriver, but it was inclined to be mucky as the black grease from the bearings always managed to spread itself over me.

Having done that job I set to work on the boltheads which protruded through the cabin roof. First I filed them down so that they were fairly smooth and then I arduously rubbed off the rust marks on the surrounding fibreglass. Then I rubbed off the rust marks on the cockpit sides where the washers on the bolts taking the tiller line blocks had rusted so badly that I suspected that they were not stainless as they should have been.

While I was doing this I leaned on the lower starboard lifeline which promptly broke. It had rusted through in secret with no external sign of decay. I replaced it with a length of green line which was just long enough to enable me to tie a knot in the end. Finally I pumped the bilge which had about six inches of water in it.

I took a sight in the morning which put me farther west than was likely. According to my noon positions that day and the day before I had covered 158 miles. A likely story. That would be an average of six and a half knots. My noon-to-noon run on the log was only 114 miles. Much more likely, considering that the wind was quite light. I didn't realize at the time how bad these fixes were; it was only on later analysis.

The wind veered and increased during the afternoon and by evening it was a boisterous Force 4 from just west of south. I shortened sail to No 3 jib and put a single reef in the mainsail. The barometer was falling steadily and I was afraid that more rough stuff was on the way.

I spent the evening re-reading *Cancer Ward* by Solzhenitsyn. Despite it being about pretty depressing conditions in Russia I enjoyed it, for it is written with humour and sensibility. I had nearly left it behind when someone told me that it was very depressing but was glad I hadn't. I didn't find it depressing, perhaps because the situation was so removed from mine.

During the night I got up to put another two reefs in the main. We still carried on at a good speed and were fairly comfortable as the sea was not very disturbed.

'However, I must say that I am getting tired of the constant motion and my thoughts turn more and more to the end of the voyage. I find that I am more apprehensive now, which is odd, as one would expect to gain rather than lose confidence.

I think that the trouble is that I am worrying more about arriving safely and in the right place.'

What I meant was that earlier in the voyage I had not considered a future different from the present, a time when I would no longer be at sea. Now I started to think of life ashore in the near future, a life of physical comfort. This made me dissatisfied with the discomfort I was now experiencing.

One does not envy people in circumstances better than one's own unless there is some expectation of improving one's lot, or some feeling that one has a right to better things. This, surely, is one of the causes of dissatisfaction in our culture. Everyone is told that all men have equal rights when it is manifest that all men do not have equal opportunities and equal abilities. Some of this dissatisfaction is justified and should be directed into changing the status quo. Much is not justified. People must direct their energies and abilities into making their own lives worthwhile and not into regretting unavoidable circumstances.

The following day, Day 35, started well with *Aziz* making good progress on the right course for America. However, during the afternoon the wind rose quickly to Force 5 and carried on rising until by midnight it was Force 7–8. I took off the jib then as we were thrashing along in a horrifying way. My nerves could not stand the frequent crashes as *Aziz* smashed her bows on to the waves. Instead we waddled along at about two knots with the main reefed to the second batten. It looked like a baggy handkerchief as it had stretched quite a lot. I could not reef farther than the second batten as the boom dropped so low that it touched the life lines. Had it been really necessary I would have had to roll a cushion in the sail to lift the boom.

The morning sea was like blue-black ink, with an occasional fleck of green as the light shone through a breaking wave. The air was a little warmer so I was back to sail changing in the nude, apart from the harness. 'I'm sure *Playboy* would love a photo!'

As I was running short of reading matter I got out my complete works of Shakespeare. I have always found it hard work reading the plays. I suppose this is due to the significance that has been invested in the plays by generations of critics, making it difficult to take them at face value and enjoy the flow of words and action. I keep stopping dead when the language is obscure. By the time I have made sense of it I have forgotten what was going on. The historical ones are worst, so I decided to pick an easy play. I lighted on *The Tempest*.

The joke didn't dawn on me until after my arrival in America. It was a peculiarly appropriate choice.

13   Trouble

It was a rough night. At 01.30 hours I thought that the wind had moderated a touch and so raised the No 3 jib. Then I went into a troubled sleep, bumping against the sides of the bunk and being woken by dollops of water falling on my head. It seemed to get rougher and rougher and after a couple of hours I could no longer stand the crashing and jerking as the bows slammed. I reluctantly climbed out of my nest and dressed up in oilskins.

I went into the cockpit and headed *Aziz* away from the wind. This eased the motion a bit but after two hours it seemed as bad as ever, so once again I climbed out. I took down the jib and left the boat moving slowly to windward. It was a pitch-black night but lightning flashed now and then showing banks of high dark cumulus. Several squalls rushed by, accompanied by torrential rain, as though someone had turned on a huge shower at full pressure, and gusts of wind whistled through the rigging.

I was putting in the top washboard to keep out the rain. I turned the wooden latch and – ouch! – squashed my middle right-hand finger. It hurt like fury for a couple of minutes and I just froze where I was, clutching my finger and letting the pain wash over me. Then it eased and became bearable. The nail was badly bruised and I hoped it would not come off. This was my most painful injury to date. I suppose I had got off lightly.

I didn't feel like sleeping after that so I switched on the radio. I picked up several local American stations on the medium band. It was quite fun listening except that they seemed to be obsessed by baseball which I did not understand at all. The reports seemed to be totally composed of jargon words which meant absolutely nothing to me, although it was all clearly of vital significance to the broadcasters. I could sympathize with American visitors to Britain during the cricket season, who listen to the conversation with a bemused and rather condescending look, as though they pity the natives who still believe in magic rites.

At 09.30 hours I raised the jib again and survived a couple of squalls, and then there was a terrific wind veer through ninety degrees. This pleased me as it meant that I could steer a course to take me a little farther south. I was worried that the almost incessant south-westerlies would push me north into the main current of the Gulf Stream. I wanted to avoid this until I was closer to America.

It was clear that I was now in the Gulf Stream and out of the rather arid sea which I had been crossing, for the phosphorescence of the water at night had increased enormously. It was a different sort of phosphorescence from that I had encountered on the way to the Azores. There it was fine-grained, a comet's tail behind the boat. Here it was a lot of quite large bright lights like glowworms, giving a spectacular burst of light as the bows crashed down and flung out a sheet of cold fire. I could watch it for hours as it formed new and ever-changing galaxies and nebulae, a visible cosmos to replace the one hidden by the overcast.

I got out Adlard Coles' *Heavy Weather Sailing*, a book which contains descriptions of some particularly bad gales and hurricanes with discussion about the tactics used in them. It has some quite horrifying pictures of waves. They frightened me so much that I hurriedly hid the book away again. I must have been quite close to the position where Humphrey Barton had his famous knockdown in *Vertue XXXV* when crossing to America. A huge wave flung the boat on to her beam ends, the doghouse smashed in and a peaceful meal was turned into a chaos of swirling water. Quick thinking and excellent seamanship saved them.

I had a minor frustration during the morning when trying to get a bath. I selected a suitably wet-looking squall, undressed and stood under its shower covering myself with liquid detergent. I had just got myself nicely soaped and was about to rinse off when the rain stopped. There I was covered with nasty sticky slime. I tried to wipe it off with paper towels without much success. Fortunately another squall arrived fairly soon and I was able to rinse off. I felt nice and clean; a pleasant change from the stickiness of sea water.

I began to recognize the pattern of weather. It was roughly as follows:

Rain, gradually increasing in intensity, followed by wind gradually increasing.

Then, suddenly, torrential rain and high wind which veers sharply. The sea is completely subdued and looks like steaming, rolling hills. Visibility is fifty yards or so.

Gradually the sky lightens and the wind eases, followed by the rain. The wind drops completely and the boat rolls horribly in a flat calm, the boom thrashing from side to side.

After a while the wind comes up again, usually from its original direction.

The whole process lasts ten to twenty-five minutes. 'I am getting a bit blasé about these occurrences now, though I still get up and watch what is going on. It is going to be a bind if it is like this all the way across the Gulf Stream. However, it could be worse. Like a hurricane!'

I kept having to haul the log line in to remove weed from it. There was still plenty of weed about and now it seemed to collect in tablecloth-size pieces instead of tea-tray or dinner-plate size. There was frequently some round the self-steering oar. I couldn't get it off easily so would wait for it to come off of its own accord, as it always did. It didn't come off the log line and when quite a bit collected it caused a terrific drag, as though we were towing a sea anchor.

The log was no longer working well, and I wondered if the strain had damaged the mechanism. The line no longer revolved gently all the time but would wait until it was fully wound up. Then it would whizz round at top speed for about half a minute before stopping to rewind itself. Perhaps it just needed oiling. I expect I lost a few miles from the record because of this.

The day passed with a number of squalls. The sea was not particularly large, perhaps eight feet. In the afternoon I was looking at the clouds when I saw a grey shiny round object high above me. It seemed to be moving against the wind, but I guess that was an illusion. I couldn't imagine what it was. A flying saucer? I concluded that it must have been a meteorological balloon. It was funny seeing a man-made object up there.

In the evening I saw a small ship approaching. He seemed to be heading for me so I went out and took over the steering. However he passed safely a few hundred yards astern. In spite of thinking he had seen me I made no attempt to communicate as conditions were such that I didn't want to get close to him. Anyway, since the *Lash Turkiye* incident I had become nervous of ships.

Had it been an emergency I would have tried to speak to him, but it would have been difficult to avoid one of us drifting down on the other with consequent damage to me. I wished again for an MIK signal.

That night I was finally forced out of the quarter berth as it had become too sodden for comfort. I moved on to the saloon berth. This had the disadvantage that one needed a leeboard when on the starboard tack to stop one arriving slowly or suddenly on the cabin floor. Instead of using the canvas leeboard which was stowed under the mattress I used the table, which bridges the berth. This proved quite satisfactory. I was much more comfortable now and happily ignored the water which fell where my head had been.

At 01.00 hours the wind had increased to a steady Force 6 and I took the jib off, allowing *Aziz* to wallow along at about one and a half knots about sixty degrees off the wind. The sky was clear and there was a spectacular display of lightning round the horizon. It was not close enough to be audible, which was a relief. I still had not got used to the idea of being the highest object in miles, just right for a lightning strike.

I slept quite well, despite the howling wind and rocking boat, and in the morning felt sufficiently confident to raise the No 3 jib. I was fed up with the slow progress that I had been making and thought that the wind had eased somewhat.

Alas, at 10.20 hours I was hit by a terrific squall with what I described in the log as hurricane-force winds – certainly an exaggeration. But I should think that the gusts definitely reached Force 9 and probably Force 10. *Aziz* was laid right over and I scrambled into the cockpit to ease off the sheets, cursing the fact that I had become too casual about squalls. I looked forward and noticed a halliard tail flying horizontally from the mast. Hang on! – that's a funny place for a halliard to come from. I glanced over the rigging and realized with a groan that the port after lower shroud was not there. Hell!

I let go the sheets and *Aziz* stopped dead, lying broadside to the wind, the sails flapping and cracking. I rushed up to the mast, not stopping for safety harness, dropped the mainsail and let go the jib halliard. I fought the jib into a bundle and stuffed it against the pulpit and lifelines. Then I hurried below to fetch the sail ties. I flipped one round the jib and then crudely bundled the mainsail on to the boom, quite a job as the boom was swinging wildly, its end frequently dipping into the seas. As soon as the sail was tied down I hauled the boom central. Then I went forward to look at the shroud.

It had broken at the bottom where the wire was round a metal thimble. A single strand had unwound from the top, suggesting that all was not well up there. I twisted the loose wire into the halliards to stop it swinging around and went below for a cigarette, a whisky, and a think.

Conditions were bad. The wind was a good Force 7, gusting 8 or 9, and the waves were very large – about fifteen or twenty feet, I estimated, trying not to overstate things. The sea was a greeny grey with white icing, and the rigging was howling as the wind roared through it.

It was a piece of luck that the shroud had broken at the bottom. A least I wouldn't have to climb the mast with the boat rolling furiously. The bottom of the shroud had been attached to the rigging screw by a pin through a loop in the end of the wire. This loop was formed by taking the wire round a metal former and squeezing a metal sleeve over the two parts. The wire had broken at the base of the loop so the sleeve was still left attached to the wire.

I decided that the best solution would be to take the wire round a block and lash it in position with thin Terylene line. The sleeve would stop the end of the wire from pulling through the lashing, with luck. I would attach the block to the rigging screw with several turns of the same Terylene line and then tighten up the screw to tension the shroud. I couldn't see any snags. I would try to get up the mast when the boat was tossing about less violently and put a rope on as an additional shroud.

I went out and completed the repair without any hitches. *Aziz* was pitching and rolling a lot but not many waves were breaking over her. I tidied up the deck and went below to take stock of the situation.

Now that I had no immediate work to do the shock of what had happened hit me. I was worried that conditions would get worse and that the rigging would not stand up. I imagined *Aziz* dismasted and washed by breaking seas.

I started to think about what would happen if I had to abandon ship. Even if I did attract the attention of a ship either by radio or by red distress flares I did not see what she could do. How would they get me aboard, and what would happen to *Aziz*. It would be too tough to attempt to take her aboard, but they couldn't just leave her to float around, a menace to shipping. Perhaps they would deliberately run her down. I visualized the boat and all my possessions sinking through the quiet dark world to crumble under the pressure of water and lie on the bottom, a sad, twisted relic of a failure. Poor *Aziz*! And poor me! Not a heroic way to end such a splendid venture.

But worse, suppose I had to take to the life raft. How long could I survive if no one found me? It would take at least two months to drift back to Europe and that was rather too long, for even if my body survived I doubted whether my mind would.

I started to think about death in a new way. Never before had I faced the prospect of imminent decease and I didn't like the idea. It may have been an unwarranted fear but it was none-theless real. Before I set out on this journey I had felt that one must die sometime and that to die during an exploit like this would be a splendid way of going. I certainly did not think that now. I was upset by the thought of missing the present and future friendships that I could see awaiting me and felt that it would be intolerable to die without having enjoyed what life has to offer. I thought now of the old people about whom it is said – they have nothing to live for. I could imagine the sadness of those who approach death still wanting to live. I did not fear the physical act of dying, but I did not want to be dead, for I have no certainty of a life after death, no feeling that there is something to look forward to.

I sat in the cabin feeling desolate.

14 Temptation Two

It blew hard all day and the seas were like rocky mountains, large, jagged and majestic. They seemed to have increased in size and I presumed that the wind had been blowing over a considerable distance to have generated so large a sea. *Aziz* was lying ahull, pointing south-east and drifting slowly north-east.

I sat in the cabin smoking furiously, unable to concentrate on anything for more than a few minutes at a time. I wished I had never heard of sailing.

At last it seemed that the wind had eased and at 20.15 hours I raised the reefed mainsail. Twenty minutes later I took it down smartly as another burst of wind struck the boat. A couple of hours later the wind really had moderated and I raised the main with its three reefs and hoisted the storm jib. *Aziz* seemed quite happy now and we progressed well. While setting the jib I was cheered to see a pretty blue fish with a yellow tail swimming just below the surface. It was about three feet long, and quite active.

I hove to twice in the night when squalls arrived for I was worried that the shroud would not stand the strain. There was terrific lightning again but it was quite a way off and I hoped that things were improving. I kept going steadily till noon the next day and thought the wind was dying away. There was still a howling from the rigging and I couldn't remember if it always howled and I hadn't noticed it earlier on or whether the wind really was still strong. I found that I had lost confidence in my judgement of conditions. I was not certain how bad things really were. Looking back I think that my estimates were about right – if anything I was underestimating.

In the morning I did so stupid a thing that I was tempted not to record it. I cut the log rotator adrift. What happened was that I had hauled in the line and found a particularly magnificent bundle of weed wrapped round it. After taking a photograph of it I started to pull it off by hand but it was rather tough so I got out my knife and started cutting it off. I was foolishly reckless in my knife work and instead of cutting the weed I sliced through the line. The whole lot fell overboard, log rotator included. I blushed at my carelessness. I had no spare so from now on I would have to estimate my speed. This meant that my dead reckoning of progress would be even less accurate than before.

At noon I unrolled a reef from the main, but soon had to roll it in again for the wind started to rise again and by midafternoon was back to Force 7. I took down the main and kept going slowly with only the storm jib.

I was rather uncertain about my position for I had not been able to get a decent sight for a couple of days, and was not very sure of my rate and direction of drift when lying ahull or sailing with a very small sail area. However, I was not close enough to the coast to be very worried and I knew that I must try to head about due west to counteract the north-easterly set of the current. This Gulf Stream current runs quite fast at its maximum – well over thirty miles a day – but it is difficult to know where it is running at that speed. I was hoping to cross it at right angles so as to get through as quickly as possible, and regretted that the bad weather made it so difficult to hold a course. Moving so slowly meant that the current had a greater effect on the direction made good.

I put up the main again that evening and we pounded along. Three hours later came a terrific slam which threw bottles all over the place from a box on the port forward berth. I promptly dropped the main before clearing up the mess.

A jam jar had smashed in the well of cans, smearing them with jam and broken glass. A bottle of disinfectant had shattered into little pieces on the floor, the liquid running into the bilge. The cabin smelled like a public lavatory. I tried to clear up all the glass as I didn't want to cut my feet. I didn't pump the bilge as I rather enjoyed the new smell, although I soon got used to it and didn't notice it. At least, I thought, it will cover the smell of mildew and dirty clothes when I arrive in America.

'20 July, Day 39. 01.00 hours. I am sitting here with a brandy and orange juice cocktail and a cigarette in my hand, pretending that I am somewhere else than this particular corner of the Atlantic. I can just visualize myself in the Griffin at Dale with a bitter in one hand and a whisky on the table and plenty of good company.

'I am beginning to think that these high winds are perpetual. If that is so I am not sure what strategy to adopt. It might be better in the long run to go south-east out of the stream and then go west nearly to the coast before going south. But that would be a long way round, and if I can make even forty miles a day directly I will do better. It may be that I am only making due north, in which case I shall wait until I am in the Labrador current and then tack down. I can't really abort to any other port as I don't have any detail charts for them.

'It might be quicker to go back to England!'

The last remark was not entirely frivolous. I was tired of the continual struggle to make headway against the wind. If I could only make forty miles a day towards America, which is against wind and current, I would be able to make 120 miles a day downwind and current. I would be able to reach Europe as quickly as America, and it would certainly be more comfortable.

I was quite tempted. It would solve the problem of how to get myself and *Aziz* back from America. But then I thought that no one would believe how close I had got. Anyway, I like to do what I have said I will do. I was damned if I would be called a failure, having got so far. I could just hear the patronizing sympathy from the men. 'Jolly good effort,' they would say, adding mentally – 'for a woman.'

But the real reason why I couldn't go back was that I knew that I couldn't live with my own cowardice. I am not brave enough to be a coward.

'It is as bad as ever today, if not worse. The sea is very confused and the wind must be a Force 8.

'I think I shall go mad if it doesn't stop soon. I have already shed tears of frustration and depression, and prayed for calm weather.

'Most of the time I just lie down and either read, listen to the radio or do nothing. It is very depressing and worrying.'

I think I was in a state of mild shock. I sat for quite long periods in a daze, something which I do not usually do.

That evening a squall came along and with a vicious tug the jib sheet pulled the sheet lead out of the track. This is the block which is mounted on a slide which can be moved along a track down the side of the boat to alter the angle that the sheet makes with the sail. The smaller the foresail the farther forward on the track must be the block. What had happened was that the eye holding the block to the slide had pulled out.

At first I thought of screwing an eye in the middle of the track as a compromise for all sheeting positions, but it was no good. I couldn't undo any of the screws holding the track down. I couldn't easily drill through the stainless-steel track under the circumstances, and there wasn't sufficient width of wood under the track for me to screw into. I ended up by screwing the eye just aft of the track and making a chain of shackles from the base of the stanchion at the forward end of the track. I put a snap shackle on the sheet block so that I could easily transfer it from one position to the other. I used the shackle chain for the storm, No 3 and No 2 jibs, and the eye for the No 1 jib and the genoa. It worked quite well, but the stanchion groaned horribly under the strain.

There was quite a lot of wind during the night, which I spent under storm jib alone. I didn't raise the main until 13.00 hours the next day by which time the wind had eased to Force 4–5, when I put on the No 3 jib and two reefs in the main.

I took a couple of sights and the position they gave put me about 360 miles from Newport. This was quite encouraging, for if the weather remained less beastly than it had been I might be able to get there in four or five days. It was now 21 July, so I might be in on the 25th or 26th.

The barometer was the highest it had been for days, but the weather was a bit erratic with a number of squalls interspersed with blue sky. The wind piped up again in the evening and I put back the storm jib and put another reef in the main.

At midnight I hove to for the night. I had the best display of lightning yet, making the whole sky a curtain of vivid lilac. There was no moon and I couldn't see when squalls were coming. This was a nuisance as I didn't dare carry much canvas lest I be caught unawares and have the shroud go again. There was plenty of rain and I caught a bowlful which tasted delicious.

In the morning the wind was down to Force 4–5 and I put on the No 3 jib. We went along at a good speed and I thought that we were getting on nicely towards America.

After lunch I was sitting in the cabin reading and trying not to notice the slamming of the bows on the waves when I was jerked to consciousness by an extra loud bang. I thought nothing of it for a second but then heard something scraping down the side of the boat. You have never seen anyone get out on deck so fast. An object was floating in my wake, looking as though it was a cube of concrete about four feet along each side. I can't imagine what it was. There didn't seem to be anything else floating around so I went below to inspect for damage. Tins and bottles went flying as I cleared the stores from where the crash seemed to have come. No sign of a leak. Whew!

This was the first, and the largest, of a number of objects I hit as I approached the American coast. The others were small pieces of wood and the occasional plastic can. I saw some large baulks of wood but managed to avoid them, for which I was duly grateful. I think the fibreglass hull would have survived a head-on collision, although the rigging might well have snapped with the shock. More danger comes from having driftwood thrown sideways into the boat in heavy weather.

'Day 41, 14.00 hours. It is very depressing to find that in spite of all my efforts I don't seem to have got very far west. And I really have no idea what my latitude is. I think the current must be stronger here than the hydrographic chart shows.

'I feel as though I am the *Flying Dutchman*, doomed for ever to sail and never make a port.'

There was a magnificent halo round the sun that afternoon,

the best I have ever seen. It was quite eerie with its pallid spectrum. Soon cloud came up and I knew that a frontal system was on its way, so I kept my fingers crossed that it would be mild. The wind was about Force 5 and *Aziz* was hopping along like a kangaroo. I suppose the wave length was just wrong for her.

That night I felt sufficiently happy to cook myself a really magnificent macaroni bolognese. I ate the lot and felt bloated. I fancied some fizzy 'pop' but had finished it all a few days earlier and had to make do with beer. I laughed at this, for I could imagine the men regretting that the beer was finished and they had to drink pop.

The bad weather kept away and by morning I had actually gone so far as to unreef the main for a Force 3 wind. Things were really looking up.

15   Nearly There

At last I was making decent progress towards the right side of the Atlantic. This was the forty-second day, the day on which I had hoped to arrive. Before I left Britain I had estimated that the voyage would take six weeks. This was worked out by assuming an average speed through the water of 100 miles a day and a distance through the water of 4,200 miles. This was a rather vague estimate as speed and distance would depend so much on the weather. I thought that if I were very lucky I might do it in five weeks and if I were unlucky it would take seven weeks.

I had requested that no search be made for me until I had been at sea for sixty days, for I did not want to cause a lot of trouble just because I had been a less successful sailor than I had hoped. Now at least I was saved that embarrassment, for I was quite close, and something serious would have to happen to prevent me arriving within the next week. My noon-to-noon run was only sixty miles, but it was all in the right direction so I felt quite confident that I would not cause too much worry to my family and friends at home.

I had a busy afternoon preparing the boat for coastal waters. The biggest job was routing out the anchors. The main anchor, a thirty-pound Danforth, was stowed in the forward cabin at the far end of the berths, with the stock lying centrally between the mattresses. It was quite a business getting it out, for I had to clear away all the stores, boxes and spare sails that were lying on top of it.

The first things out were the remaining eggs, about three dozen of them, still packed in their fragile plastic boxes. They went rapidly overboard as I was using so few that it didn't seem worth keeping more than half a dozen. They were hastily followed by several vacuum packs of bacon which should have been opened more than a month earlier, and had started to putrify. In spite of the thick polythene packs I could smell the contents. Then I piled everything into the corners of the berths and wedged myself into a position where I could get hold of the anchor.

It was quite a fight. I tried to lift it out but because I was in such an awkward position I couldn't get enough leverage on it. I crawled on to the berths, my feet on the tins in the well and tried again. I got it partly out, but the crosspiece jammed under the mattress. I heaved again, and it came loose with a rush, and I nearly fell into the tins. I dragged it towards me, balanced it on the edge of the bunk, and wormed myself backwards until I was standing on the main cabin floor. Finally, sweating profusely, I lifted it down and put it on the only clear floor space, just by the steps leading to the cockpit.

I then got out the twenty-pound Danforth anchor from the lower stowage, a much easier job as it was a lot smaller. I took the three fathoms of chain which were on this anchor and shackled it on to the big one. Then I took the fathom of chain off the fifteen-pound plough anchor which was stowed in the bilge and shackled that on to the twenty-pounder.

After that bit of musical chairs I got the two anchor warps from the after stowage and shackled one to each anchor. Now was the opportunity to do what I had never seen done but is always recommended: mark off the twenty-five-fathom warps in lengths, so that you can tell how much is out when anchoring instead of estimating by eye. I did this by tying lengths of parachute cord at three-fathom intervals, and this seemed quite easy to understand by feel as well as by eye.

The most entertaining job I did that day was hoisting the Dale Yacht Club burgee to the masthead. I had taken it down some time before as it was fraying, but felt that now was the time to show the flag again. I had flown the Little Ship Club burgee all the time at the starboard crosstree and it had survived, though decidedly tattered.

The problem about raising the burgee was that the halliard

and block were on the windward side of the mast. Each time I tried to finish hoisting, the burgee stick would either jam against the masthead fittings or under the backstay. I tried hoisting the last few feet very quickly, at the same time giving a hefty flick to windward, but without success, and after I had almost got the stick permanently stuck in the shrouds I gave up. I brought *Aziz* into the wind where she hung in stays until I finished the job and relatched the self-steering on course. She looked much better with the red and green burgee flying and I felt decently dressed for any meeting with other boats.

I rewarded myself with a brandy and lemon juice. One of the advantages of having the chronometer on Greenwich Mean Time and the alarm clock on local time, about four hours earlier, was that I could always justify eating or drinking at any time, as on one time or the other it was appropriate. I had sauté potatoes for supper, the best so far. I was now getting the hang of cooking them, and felt that if I had learned nothing else from the crossing this single skill was a worthwhile achievement.

The night was peaceful but there were more squalls the next morning and I put a reef in the main. They can't have been much of squalls to warrant only one reef. Nevertheless they looked impressive. I wrote in the log 'towering leaden cumulus marching across the sky trailing streamers of rain, and each bearing a tightly packed bag of wind'. They soon marched away, leaving a Force 2 south-westerly breeze, and I unreefed and put on the No 1 jib. This was the first time for ten days that I had had the No 1 up, so I felt that things were really going well.

I managed to pick up a radio signal which I thought was from the Nantucket Shoals Light Vessel. It was rather faint but the bearing was reasonable, though not accurate enough for navigation. But it was evidence that the charts were telling the truth when they said that there was land just over the horizon. 'It is funny to think that I am actually going to see land in a day or two; and a land of fables and myths to me, a mere Britisher.'

It rained that evening, a gentle rain like that in England instead of the spitting showers we had been having. The barometer was falling once again and I hoped the weather wasn't going to play another nasty trick on me. I could see a lot of birds about, most of them Leach's petrels, a few storm petrels, and a number of birds which looked like black gulls.

By evening I had made enough progress to be able to get a radio DF bearing on the Nantucket Shoals Light Vessel, but I got rather a shock when I plotted it.

'I seem to be way out on my navigation. According to a DF bearing on Nantucket I am nearly fifty miles west of where I thought. Something has gone seriously wrong somewhere.'

But then:

'I have just taken a sight with the sun very low, but it figures well with the DF. Actually I wasn't nearly as far out as I said – I had forgotten to transfer the fix earlier today. Even so, I am a bit out, but not half as bad as I thought. At present we are about twenty-five miles south of the light vessel.'

I was in fact only fifteen miles out, which was not bad considering the ropiness of my sextant and DF apparatus which was all noise and not much signal. I had a terrible job taking bearings with it, as it was difficult to pinpoint the position of minimum signal strength. I think the transistors must have been passing away.

At dusk that night, which was about 23.00 hours GMT, I sailed about a quarter of a mile from a stationary vessel. Only when it was to windward of me did I discover to my chagrin that it was a Coast Guard vessel. I was not inclined to beat back to it for a chat, particularly as it was getting dark, but as I went quite close I thought they would have noticed me. They never did report me which was a pity.

At about 02.30 hours, in a pitch-black night, I picked up the loom of the light vessel exactly where I expected it to be. Very gratifying for I had not thought that I would be close enough to see it. I was approaching the separation lanes for shipping in and out of New York, so I spent the night having quick snatches of sleep and keeping watch. I didn't see much shipping but suspect that mist came down earlier than I realized, blocking out the lights. When light came I could see that it was very misty, almost foggy. We were within soundings of my thirty-fathom echo sounder, and the sea had changed to a cold bottle green quite different from the warm Gulf Stream blue.

I had difficulty getting a radio bearing on the light vessel for some reason, but was soon able to get bearings from several beacons on the coast. There was practically no wind and I spent the day alternately drifting and trickling along. I heard on the radio station at Providence that they expected fog that night and the following morning, which was disappointing, though hardly surprising. The frequency of fog in these waters is very high.

I spent quite a time trying to make the port navigation light work, as it hadn't lit up when I asked it to the previous night. When I unscrewed the cover I discovered that the top of the bulb holder had corroded away where I had put an aluminium rivet in it shortly after buying the boat. I had to do a botch job with a spare bulb from the compass stuck up with wire and insulating tape. It worked adequately.

Half an hour before midnight I saw a whale playing about 300 yards away. I was very surprised, for I had not realized that they came into such shallow water. I was pleased to see one there for it indicated that the water was by no means as polluted as I had been led to believe. And that the great whaling fleets of New England had not completely wiped out their victims.

I was now getting quite close to land and hoped I would see some sign of it before morning. I took an anti-sleep pill and prepared for a long night of watchkeeping and navigation.

In the middle of the night, local time, I saw a vessel heading straight for me. I couldn't make head or tail of his lights; he seemed to have them the wrong way round. He came quite close and I flashed him D – keep clear, I am having difficulty in manoeuvring. This was an understatement for I was completely becalmed and could not even keep *Aziz* pointing in the same direction.

I heard the engines die abruptly, and he came slowly past to have a look at me. I heard a voice exclaim with surprise, 'Hey, it's a sailboat.' As he came by I could see that he was a fishing vessel about fifty feet long, with a forward white masthead light and his red and green navigation lights on the wheelhouse sides at the rear. No wonder I had been confused; ships carry their navigation lights in front of their masthead lights.

I shouted across and asked if he would tell me my position, and heard a surprised reaction to my voice, whether because it was a woman's voice or because of my English accent I don't know. He did a circuit and came back to tell me that I was ten miles due south of No Man's Land, which figured with my estimates.

I told him that I had come non-stop from Britain and asked him to notify the Coast Guard that I was here. He seemed to have difficulty understanding me, and was quite lost when I spelled out the name of my boat. I discovered later that Americans don't say 'zed', but 'zee'.

The boat finally chugged off leaving me happy, knowing where I was and that I had made contact with America.

16 Discovering America

It was the most frustrating night of the voyage. The wind was light and fitful, never deciding whence it came, never even deciding if it existed. I spent hours at the helm trying to keep *Aziz* pointing in the right direction, watching the stars spin above the mast as she drifted round and round. The surface of the water was shrouded in mist and, as the dawn broke, the sun rose dramatically from the haze, a glowing red ball, molten metal in an oily sea.

Aziz crept idly on in the mist as I watched the cats' paws ruffling the sea as they passed by. Shortly after dawn I had a harbinger of land: a little green leaf beetle settled on the cabin roof and crawled inquisitively over my hand as I removed it to a safer place. Land birds flew overhead on urgent missions from island to island.

I tried to start the engine but found that the battery was too flat to turn it over. I had not the strength to do so by hand. If I had started it I would have had to fix it permanently in gear for the gear cable had rusted through. Still, that was irrelevant. At last I sighted evidence of man's presence in these foreign waters, a row of fishing buoys each with a flag hanging limply round its stick. At first I was afraid that I was close to shore, but the depth of water was still over a hundred feet so I guessed that there were lobster pots below me.

The mist was quite thick now, and I could hear a foghorn calling urgently to port. I replied with my aerosal horn, deafening myself every minute. Soon a dark shape congealed from the mist and a small ship thumped across my bows a few hundred yards away. This was my first indication of visibility in this mist and I realized that I would have little warning of land. I thanked my lucky stars that the tides do not run strongly in this area, for I had little control of where I was going.

I spent much of the time taking radio bearings from the various beacons in the locality. The radio was so noisy that the fixes showed as large polygons on the large-scale chart. However, I was confident that I was still no closer than ten miles from the nearest land, either Block Island or Martha's Vineyard. At about 10.00 hours local time I was taking a set of bearings when I heard a noisy engine approaching. I popped out and saw a cabin cruiser going like a bat out of hell from west to east. I waved and brandished the loudhailer. They waved back and were soon lost in the mist.

A few minutes later I heard another engine, and out of the mist came another cabin cruiser. Again I waved and brandished my loudhailer and the boat slowed down, and came to rest close by. She was the *Edlor III* of New York, a smart cruiser about thirty feet long and, to my delight, carrying a large and businesslike radio aerial. A man and woman were aboard and asked me what I wanted. I explained that I was non-stop from Europe to Newport and asked that he report me to the Coast Guard, which he did.

They asked if I needed anything and I said, half joking, that I wouldn't mind a tow, and after the captain of the *Edlor* had answered numerous questions about himself, and a few about me, the Coast Guard said they would send out a boat. They also passed the information that my parents were in Newport awaiting my arrival, which was a terrific piece of news, for before I left they had said that they would not come to meet me as they would not know when I would arrive. I was very pleased, for I knew how much they would enjoy my success.

The *Edlor* stayed with me waiting for the Coast Guard boat, and after getting dizzy sailing round and round her I tied up astern and, after changing into a mini dress and tidying up a bit, went aboard. Ed Hollowell and his wife Lorna were on their way back to New York after a week's cruising. They gave me lunch of beer and ham and cheese sandwiches. Real bread! Though it didn't taste like English bread I thoroughly enjoyed it. I don't know what we talked about but I was blissfully happy.

It was odd to see *Aziz* from the outside, for she had become a part of me. She looked so large and yet so small and I could hardly believe that she had brought me all the way from Europe. I was pleased that she was looking quite smart, apart from a few rust stains, and I congratulated her on her performance over the past six weeks.

After about an hour and a half the Coast Guard boat arrived and took me in tow. I waved goodbye to the *Edlor*, and we set off at a terrific speed. I nearly had a fit, for a huge standing wave was set up with a terrific trough amidships, and I feared that the strain might be too great for *Aziz*. It would be a pity if she broke up now. I hooted the foghorn and explained that it was too fast, and we set off again at a more moderate pace. I took the opportunity to clear up the inside of the boat and then sat on deck, a can of beer in one hand, a cigarette in the other and an idiot grin all over my face. I retired to the shelter of the cabin only when it started to drizzle.

After a while we arrived close to the Brenton Reef light structure, a Meccano sculpture rising from the sea about two miles from the entrance to Narragansett Bay. The light was flashing and the foghorn howled mournfully. I was cast adrift there and told that another boat would pick me up. The atmosphere darkened, the heavens opened, thunder cracked and I was soaked with rain. It did not prevent me smiling happily at photographers who were firing their cameras at me from a motor boat.

Soon there appeared out of the mist a boat with a flashing blue light on top, and I was taken in tow. We set off for the last few miles to Newport. I stood on deck waving at the photographers and the Coast Guard, my heart almost bursting with joy. Quite suddenly I realized that land was visible, a blue-grey shore line a few hundred yards away.

I really have made it! There really is land over here. America is not an imaginary land, but a real place. Now I know how Christopher Columbus felt – a great sense of pride and achievement.

Soon more boats appeared and formed an escort. Although the rain was pouring down I stripped off my oilskins for the

Coast Guard shouted that I was expected to be wearing hot pants. I felt that the mini dress was a good substitute for them, and stood there soaked from head to toe and enjoying every minute. A large motor yacht joined the formation and I was told that it belonged to the Mayor of Newport.

At about four o'clock local time we came round a headland and there was Newport harbour, with plenty of yachts at anchor and moored along the quays. As we entered foghorns were sounded. A marvellous welcome for someone who had been worried that no one would be expecting her. I stood on the cabin roof, clinging to the mast, quite bemused by it all. *Aziz* was brought alongside a pontoon at the Port O' Call marina, and there were my parents, with happy smiles on their faces.

I embraced them and helped them aboard, where we posed for photographs. Then we went below with the Customs Officer, who rapidly dealt with my passport and collected my remaining fresh fruit and vegetables which he took away to burn. These formalities over I stepped on to the pontoon, posed for more photographs, said a few words into a microphone and then climbed a ramp and set foot on dry land.

I was surrounded by friendly and enthusiastic people, all asking questions. I replied as best I could, which was not very well (under the circumstances) for I was too excited to think clearly. Then my parents and I were driven to a hotel on Goat Island, where we were well looked after. It was there that I had my first of very few disappointments in America. The bath was too short for me to lie basking comfortably. Still, it was marvellous to soak in hot fresh water.

That evening I was feeling so fit and happy that I went to two parties and then to someone's house for steak and salad. Delicious. When we arrived back at the hotel at about half past midnight local time, which seemed much later to me because I was still used to Greenwich time, which was five hours later, a television camera crew were waiting to interview me. Friends who saw the interview told me that I had already picked up an American accent. If I had it was because I was enjoying American hospitality so much.

Next day was hectic. I spent the morning running between the two telephones in my room, answering questions, posing for photographers. I was happy to talk to anyone and everyone, Press and well wishers. I recorded several telephone interviews with the BBC, which was fun, although after a time I found that I was saying the same thing over again.

I spent five days in Newport, and enjoyed every minute. It is a beautiful city, one of the oldest in America, and the houses have great character. The Mayor, Fred Alofsin, was most hospitable. He took my parents and me round the harbour on his motor yacht and gave us a splendid dinner at a quayside restaurant. Then he asked me to go along to a City Council meeting one evening. I went along, not knowing what to expect, and was quite overwhelmed to be made an Honorary Citizen of Newport, and by an impressive declaration that 26 July 1971 be known henceforth as Nicolette Milnes Walker Day.

We were also well entertained by the officers of HMS *Jupiter*, which was visiting Newport Naval Base. They gave me a huge Union Jack which I flew at the masthead of *Aziz*; strictly non-etiquette, but a splendid show, for it was visible almost all over Newport.

The Newport Chamber of Commerce gave me a champagne reception at the marina, and presented me with a splendid inscribed silver salver.

I had one worry: *Aziz*. I could not afford to have her shipped back to England, for that would cost at least £1,000, so I set about trying to sell her. Various people expressed interest and I was hopeful that a sale could be arranged, when I received a telegram from the Esso Petroleum Company in London. They wished to buy the boat, transport her to England and put her on display at the World Sportacular Show at Earls Court, which I was invited to open jointly with Chay Blyth, whose boat *British Steel* would also be on show. I accepted gladly, for I had not wanted to leave *Aziz* in America, far from home.

Then I received an invitation from Cunard to travel back to England as their guest on the *Queen Elizabeth II*. This was great, for I wanted to travel back by sea to have another look at the ocean, this time from something big and safe. My mother and I rushed to the shops to buy clothes more suited to such a crossing than those I had brought with me.

Five days after arriving in Newport I said goodbye to my parents and they returned to England by air. I was driven across Connecticut to Westchester, the county just north of New York City, and across Westchester to Scarborough, a leafy suburb, where I was to stay with Sol Stein, who is publishing this book in America.

In Scarborough I worked with Sol on the plan for this book, trying to catch my thoughts and feelings while they were fresh. I also had time to see a little of American life. I visited the shopping centre there and was amazed to discover a shop which sold twenty something different sorts of ice-cream. I was shown round the area, and was very impressed by the way the houses were tucked away among the trees. Instead of chopping the vegetation away it had been left to enhance the attraction of the area.

I liked what I saw of America. I had found it much more attractive than I had expected, and had found the people not just chummy but genuinely friendly. I took great delight in the surprised reaction of many people when first meeting me. Clearly they expected a large, strong, horsey-faced English girl, long in tooth. Instead I was a small, apparently frail, round-faced girl, a teenage imposter.

I visited Manhattan for a day and was amazed by it. The chrome-plated parts were OK, but I was staggered to see such poor housing and rotten buildings within a stone's throw of these shiny parts. I crossed on the Staten Island ferry and saw the famed Manhattan skyline, but also the soupy water full of debris. But whatever the fabric of America may be like, the people I met were great. Of course, ten days is not much time to judge a place, though many commentators do with less, and I was seeing it from a rather unusual viewpoint, but I was quite won over from my mild British anti-Americanism, and am looking forward to my next visit.

And so, ten days after arriving in America, I again put out

to sea. This time not alone, but in the company of about 2,000 people. Instead of a thirty-foot sailing boat I was on a steam-turbine powered ocean liner 963 feet in length.

The ocean remained a child of immense power and quick temper. I was glad that I would be able to salute him, and thank him for ignoring the impertinence of my challenge. I respect the masterful Atlantic and am pleased that he respected my determination to make my voyage in pursuit of a chance of freedom.

17 Taking the Crown

The crossing on the *Queen Elizabeth* was my initiation into the public life I would have to face from now on. I sat on the Captain's right at dinner, which was a great honour and a pleasure for me. I was invited to many cocktail parties which I was delighted to go to as I met so many different people. Everyone was very kind to me, but I confess that at times I felt rather like a goldfish in a bowl, unable to hide from the surrounding eyes.

I was amused by the differing behaviour of the British and American passengers. The latter would come up to me, shake my hand and congratulate me on my achievement, but on the whole the British stood off, looking at me surreptitiously and muttering among themselves. Of course I exaggerate, but some such pattern was evident.

The crossing was very calm, which was a disappointment to me, though not to most of the passengers. I had hoped to see some big waves and strong winds so that I could compare them with what I had experienced in *Aziz*. The sea looked quite different from a height of forty feet or more, crawling beneath one instead of surging round. The feeling of being a part of the ocean was quite lost. Now I was only an observer, not a participator.

The liner ploughed across the waters at more than thirty miles an hour, and five and a half days after leaving New York we docked in Southampton at midnight. The following morning I was faced with a Press conference, which took a long time. Robin Knox-Johnston, the first man to sail non-stop round the world by himself, presented me with a reproduction of a painting of *Aziz*, on behalf of the builders, Southern Ocean Shipyard. We were photographed exhaustively, I recorded three television interviews and talked to a number of reporters.

The Lord Mayor of Southampton welcomed me most kindly and the Lady Mayoress presented me with a splendid bouquet. Then, after more questions and a taped interview for the BBC, I was free to talk to my family.

Rolls-Royce had put a car at our disposal and my parents and I were driven in it to a nearby hotel where the rest of the family had congregated. There were, I think, twelve of them, a small portion of my large number of relations. At last I could talk to them for a few minutes over a cup of coffee and unwind a little after the tensions of the publicity machine. Then the family scattered, returning to their respective homes, and my parents and I were driven to Newbury for lunch at my Uncle Robert's, and then back to Cheshire.

I felt then that I had really completed the round trip and come back to where I started from. But I was not allowed to forget that I had been away. A pile of letters awaited me, some just of congratulation, others requesting me to attend some function or other. I determined that I should reply to everybody who wrote to me and immediately bought an electric typewriter to help me.

What I really wanted to do was to settle down and write this book, something I was looking forward to. I eventually managed to reply to all the kind people who wrote to me, and started on my writing. It was great fun, but hard work, though as my typing improved I was able to spend more time creating and less reproducing. Eventually I gave up writing in longhand first and took to typing straight on to the page. Ten weeks after landing in England I delivered the manuscript to the publishers.

Of course, I was not allowed to hide away to write. I was now a public figure, and as such had to attend public functions. I was rather apprehensive about this at first, but I said to myself that I must deliberately set out to enjoy these occasions, or I would suffer agonies. And I have enjoyed them. I have met a great number of interesting people and been to many interesting places.

As soon as I arrived back home in Cheshire I was given a reception at the Bickerton Village Institute, where I was presented with an illuminated scroll by the Chairman of the Parish Council. This was great fun, for I was able to meet practically everybody in the village where my parents had lived for five years.

A few weeks later I was given a reception by the Nantwich Rural District Council and I had the pleasure of meeting many of the distinguished people in the area.

Shortly after my arrival back in England I opened the World Sportacular Exhibition in London, with Chay Blyth. Both my boat *Aziz* and his boat, *British Steel*, were on show. What a contrast. *British Steel* is about twice the length of *Aziz*, but looks huge by comparison, a really professional craft which had survived a great circumnavigation excellently. Chay Blyth was most charming, a likeable man without pretension, and clearly a most courageous sailor.

I cannot possibly mention all the functions I have attended, but would like to thank everyone who has entertained me for their kindness and hospitality.

It is an odd feeling, being a celebrity. How easy it would be to believe what is said about one. But often I hardly recognize myself in the glowing descriptions, and am careful to remain myself and not become the fictional public figure. I am still the woman who, less than a year ago, conceived the idea of a solo Atlantic crossing. Of course I have changed in some ways. I am more confident of myself, and therefore more able to be open and honest with myself and others. My experience of the Atlantic and the subsequent events has made me more receptive to new ideas and new experiences and my pleasure in life has been enhanced. But I remain myself, Nicolette, a twenty-eight-year-old, five-foot-four-inch, eight-stone woman. I would not wish to be anyone else.

Neither would I do the same trip again, for one cannot repeat a new experience. I don't think I would do anything alone for a long period, not because I dislike being alone but because when you share an experience with someone the experience is enhanced, both as it happens and in retrospect. I look forward to new journeys of discovery. Of discovering myself. Writing this book has been one. I am going to make sure that there are others. Now my mind has come alive I am not going to let it die.

POWER

There are few, few indeed
Who can take the crown but keep
Integrity. Some special need
Is here required. I think a deep

Knowledge of self is first of all
Essential. Then simplicity.
Wisdom, of course, always, in call.
And there we have the mastery.

ELIZABETH JENNINGS

Appendices

1 List of Stores

NAVIGATION

Ebbco plastic sextant
Old sextant
Harrison deck watch
Brookes and Gatehouse
  Direction Finding Radio
Brookes and Gatehouse
  Echo Sounder
Binoculars
Hand-bearing compass
Dinghy compass
  (used as tell-tale)
Harries protractor

Dividers
Log book
Note books
Pencils
Chinagraph pencils
Lead pencils
Ball-point pens
India rubber
Reed's Nautical Almanac
Air Almanac
Sight Reduction Tables
Walker Excelsior Log

ADMIRALTY PUBLICATIONS

List of Lights, vols D, H, J
List of Radio Signals, vols II, V
Pilots
  37 West Coast of England
  68 East Coast of United States, Vol I
  59 Nova Scotia, SE Coast and Bay of Fundy
Charts
    1 Portsmouth to Canary Isles and Azores
  4009 North Atlantic Ocean – Northern portion
  1123 South Coast of Ireland to Land's End
  3272 Newfoundland to Bermuda

CHANDLERY, ETC

6 assorted blocks

Assorted shackles

Assorted snap shackles

Assorted thimbles

2 rigging screws

Clevis pins, split rings, locking wire

10 jib hanks

2 plastic cleats

Assorted stainless-steel eyes

Assorted plastic eyes

Spare battens

Length of Tufnol-type batten material

Sail thread

Sail cloth

Needles

Palm

Sail repair tape

Insulating tape

Plastic tape

Araldite adhesive

Evostick adhesive

Wood glue

2 Isopon fibreglass repair kits

2 sq ft copper sheet

Various pieces of wood

Paint varnish

Silicon grease

Light oil

Plus Gas lubricating and protecting liquid

Combat lubricating and protecting liquid (aerosol)

Flexible sealer

Electric wire

Spare compass and navigation light bulbs

Cable clips

Hose clips

2 funnels

Whipping twine

Codline

Sparking plugs

Spare mainsheet

Spare jibsheet

2 × 25 fathom anchor warps

3 spinnaker sheets

Assorted mooring lines

15 fathoms 1-in. Terylene line

10 fathoms $1\frac{1}{4}$-in. Terylene line

10 fathoms $\frac{1}{2}$-in. Terylene line

Assorted thin Terylene line

Assorted shock cord

Canvas bosun's chair and hoisting tackle

Spare bilge pump

Spare tiller

Solar still

Tilley lamp
Assorted torches
Signalling lamp
Red and white smoke flares
Life raft
Emergency radio transmitter

Aerosol foghorn
Loudhailer
Life jacket
Safety harness
Fire extinguisher

TOOLS, ETC

2 hammers
Assorted screwdrivers
2 wood saws
Hacksaw and blades
Midget hacksaw
Small adjustable spanner
Large adjustable spanner
2 pairs pliers
1 pair pincers
Sheet metal cutters
Wood plane
Assorted files
Assorted chisels
Pop riveter and rivets

2 hand drills
3 sets drill bits
Mole wrench
Pipe wrench
Bolt cropper
Steel rule
Plug spanner
Carborundum block
Set of carving chisels
Assorted nuts, bolts and
  screws
Pocket knife
Stanley knife

FOOD AND DRINK

9 cans steak
9 cans minced beef
10 cans meatballs
9 cans spam
3 cans sausages
6 cans tuna
6 cans sardines
2 cans anchovies
3 cans cod roe
9 cans prawns

5 cans ravioli
5 cans baked beans
5 cans curried beans
12 cans potatoes
10 cans assorted vegetables
15 cans assorted fruit
1 can ham
2 cans asparagus
1 can li-chees

9 pkts Surprise peas
9 pkts Surprise beans
4 tubs dried vegetable flakes
9 dehydrated meals
12 pkts instant potato
1 lb spaghetti
3 lb quick macaroni
5 lb rice
3 lb flour
3 pkts oatmeal
5 lb black bread
10 lb sugar
5 lb dried fruit
5 lb canned butter
2 lb lard
2 bottles cooking oil
36 pts Ever Ready milk
2 cans dried milk
2 lb Nescafé
100 teabags
6 lb cheese
5 doz eggs
4 pints lemon juice
2 bottles orange squash
Assorted sauces, pickles,

herbs and spices
2 jars marmalade
2 jars jam
2 jars honey
2 jars Marmite
10 pkts Ryvita
2 tins biscuits
Mother's biscuits and cake
4 lb muesli
10 cans soup
10 pkts soup

10 lb potatoes
10 lb onions
5 lb carrots
4 doz oranges
4 doz apples
2 lemons
5 box green tomatoes
6 doz cans beer
6 bottles whisky
6 bottles brandy
12 bottles carbonated drinks
1,000 cigarettes
4 lb sweets

MISCELLANEOUS

Radio
2 cassette tape-recorders
5 recorded music tapes
5 unused tapes
Approx 40 assorted books
Sewing kit
Washing kit
Soap
Washing-up liquid detergent

Disinfectant
Shampoo
Toilet paper
Kitchen paper
Clothes pegs
2 cameras
Film
Fishing tackle
Matches

Tea towels
2 prs scissors
2 alarm clocks
Vanity case with cosmetics,
    etc

2 frying pans
1 non-stick saucepan
1 pressure cooker
1 kettle
Assorted crockery and cutlery

2 The Boat

Aziz is a Pionier-class fast cruiser-racer. This class was designed by E. G. Van de Stadt in 1959, one of the first yachts designed specifically to be built in fibreglass. The class proved successful both in offshore racing and for cruising and over 200 were built by Southern Ocean Shipyard Ltd of Poole, Dorset.

Aziz is the thirty-ninth Pionier and was built in 1963 for the late Captain Jack Sanderson of Budleigh Salterton, Devon, who was a polo player well known in both India and England. The name is Arabic and means magnificent or beautiful, and the boat was called after Captain Sanderson's favourite polo pony.

In 1969 *Aziz* was sold to Mr Ric Carpenter of Cowes, Isle of Wight, who used her for channel cruising.

I bought *Aziz* from Mr Carpenter in March 1971. She was in good condition and had clearly been looked after well. No major repairs were necessary.

The diagrams show her sail plan, accommodation layout and dimensions.

I had four major modifications made: two to strengthen the structure and two to ease single-handed sailing.

The windows, which are six feet long without a break in the plastic, were covered with plywood boards into which were set plastic portholes. I had this done because I felt that so long a window might be vulnerable if the boat were thrown on her beam ends. The after bulkhead was strengthened by the addition of solid teak beams as Brian Henshall, of the Dale Sailing Company, thought that it might not stand up to a pooping sea. The washboards were also reinforced.

A Hasler Gibbs servo pendulum self-steering gear was fitted. This involved the manufacture of a bracket to support the vane, as *Aziz* was not fitted with a stern pulpit. This bracket was

Sail Areas (in sq ft)

Genoa	250
Small Genoa	230
No 1 Jib	199
No 2 Jib	154
No 3 Jib	120
Storm Jib	68
Mainsail	174

JOHN BATCHELOR

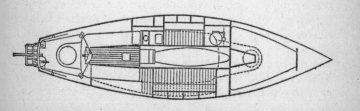

made by Dick Edwards of Dale from 1½-inch galvanized pipe and proved quite satisfactory.

Before collecting *Aziz* from Cowes I had a twin forestay fitted. This was to allow me to carry twin foresails when sailing downwind, and to allow me to keep one foresail hanked on ready for use. As it happened I rarely did this as I always seemed to have the wrong sail hanked on.

The internal arrangements were quite satisfactory and for one person there was plenty of space.

My only complaints about the design of the boat are that the forehatch was badly secured and leaked, despite being sealed all round. Because the attachment was in the centre of the circular hatch cover the cover itself was quite noticeably deformed. I would also have liked a spray rail on the cabin roof. Frequently a wave would come over the bows, up over the roof and drop into the cabin.

As regards sails I had little to complain about. I was very glad that I had acquired an extra jib to fill the gap between the working and storm jibs. It was very useful. I also think that the storm jib was too large; about forty square feet would have been better.

All the gear worked well and the only breakages I had were a shroud and the starboard jib fairlead slide. I had no difficulty handling the gear, but could not have managed without two mast winches. That for the main halliard was essential when unreefing the mainsail.

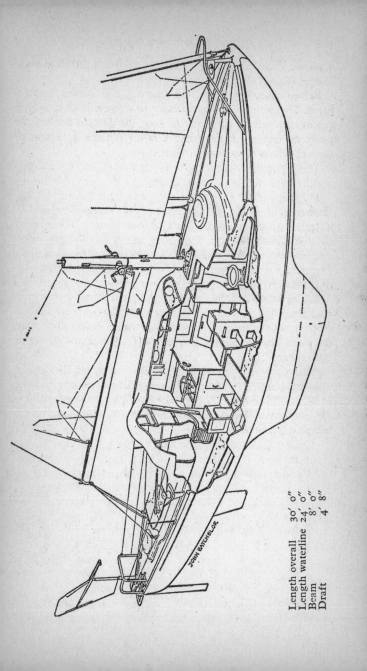

JOHN BATCHELOR

Length overall   30′ 0″
Length waterline 24′ 0″
Beam   8′ 0″
Draft   4′ 8″

3 Facts and Figures

ROUTE

I chose to go by the Azores route as I was making the crossing for pleasure and not in a race. The direct route, in my opinion, is more dangerous as well as more uncomfortable, as it takes one along the shipping lanes, across the Grand Banks with their fog and fishing fleets, and down the Canadian coast. The Azores route is away from shipping, warmer and less windy, and does not involve any long coastal passage.

I divided the route into three parts.

Part 1. The Great Circle route from St Ann's Head to a point between Sao Miguel and Terceira in the Azores, continued to latitude 37° N.

Part 2. Due West along latitude 37° N until reaching longitude 65° W. This is just south of the Gulf Stream flow.

Part 3. From 65° W a Great Circle route to Rhode Island. This allows one to cross the strong flow of the Gulf Stream where it is fairly narrow.

I did not follow this plan exactly because of weather and poor tactics. I allowed myself to get too far east of course on Part 1, and passed between Sao Miguel and Santa Maria because I did not want to beat into the westerly wind to get north of Sao Miguel. I now think it would have been better if I had done so.

In Part 2 I allowed myself to get a little far north early on, which meant I had difficulty in staying out of the Gulf Stream flow. As I approached the end of this part I allowed myself to be pushed into the Gulf Stream a bit too soon, and in the ensuing bad weather drifted east so that my course to cross the Stream was less oblique than I wanted. This meant that the current had a greater effect than it would otherwise have had.

Despite starting Part 3 from the wrong place I was able to make a good course towards land and made my landfall without trouble.

I reckoned that the divergencies from my plan cost me between two and five days. I would not change the planned route another time.

NAVIGATION

I had trouble with my sextant early on and was uncertain of my position until I picked up the Azores beacons on the radio. I discovered that the index error on the sextant was continually changing, and had to measure it each time I took a sight. After that I had no problems, and I think that my navigation gave fixes within fifteen miles of my true position at worst.

I had great difficulty in using the radio direction finding set because there was so much hiss and crackle coming through the headphones that I could not hear the signal clearly. I should have had it serviced before I set out.

The Harrison deck watch which I was using as a chronometer was a bit erratic but I was able to pick up time signals from the British or Australian broadcasting services nearly every day.

The rotating log worked well until towards the end of the crossing when the clock part seemed to stiffen up so that the line would wind itself up before spinning the clock 'winder'. I was about to oil it when I accidentally cut off the rotator, so did not bother.

The echo sounder gave me no trouble and was very useful when I was approaching land in fog.

SPEED AND DISTANCE

Distance over the ground: 3,400 nautical miles.
Average speed over the ground: 76½ miles per day.
Distance through the water: 4,000 n miles.*
Average speed through the water: 90 miles per day.*

* Estimated as the log rotator was lost late in the voyage.

Greatest day's run recorded on the log: 137 n miles.
Greatest day's run noon-to-noon by sights: 158 n miles.†
Smallest day's run recorded on the log: 28 n miles.
Smallest day's run noon-to-noon by sights: 34 n miles.
   (But also note 88 n miles in three days during the Gulf
Stream bad weather.)

SAIL CHANGES

Total mainsail changes (reefing and unreefing): 65.
Total headsail changes (including removing but not replacing
a sail): 59.

USAGE OF HEAD SAILS

Genoa	Small Genoa	No 1 jib	No 2 jib	No 3 jib	Storm jib
9	1	18	10	13	6

† Probably an overestimate, but some bonus from current gained.

Francis Chichester

GIPSY MOTH CIRCLES THE WORLD

30p

Francis Chichester, at 65 set out from Plymouth in his 53-foot ketch (Gipsy Moth IV) on 27th August 1966 and sailed first to Sydney, thence eastwards via Cape Horn, arriving back at Plymouth on 28th May 1967. A magnificent voyage that captured the imagination of the world. 'Has a part in the dreams of all of us' – THE GUARDIAN

THE LONELY SEA AND THE SKY 30p

'A really thrilling story of an adventurous, brave and successful life' – NEWS OF THE WORLD

'A gay and entertaining self-portrait of an anti-hero' – THE TIMES

Chay Blyth

THE IMPOSSIBLE VOYAGE   45p

'The most outstanding passage under sail that has ever been made by one man alone' – THE TIMES

'A thrilling tale of achievement. Blyth emerges as something unique, someone a lot larger than the majority' – SCOTSMAN

'Buoyant and humorous' – DAILY TELEGRAPH

These and other PAN Books are obtainable from all booksellers and newsagents. If you have any difficulty please send purchase price plus 7p postage to PO Box 11, Falmouth, Cornwall.

While every effort is made to keep prices low, it is sometimes necessary to increase prices at short notice. PAN Books reserve the right to show new retail prices on covers which may differ from those previously advertised in the text or elsewhere.